THE
POWER OF
THE NEW
SPIRITUALITY

Also by William Bloom

Psychic Protection
The Endorphin Effect
Feeling Safe
Encyclopedia of Mind Body Spirit (ed.)
Soulution: The Holistic Manifesto
Personal Identity, National Identity and International Relations
Money, Heart and Mind: Financial Well-Being for People and Planet
The Penguin Book of New Age and Holistic Writing (ed.)
The Holistic Revolution (ed.)
Meditation in a Changing World
Ley Lines and Ecology
Sacred Times—A New Approach to Festivals
The New Age (ed.)
The Seekers Guide (ed.)
First Steps—An Introduction to Spiritual Practice
The Sacred Magician

THE POWER OF THE NEW SPIRITUALITY

How to Live a Life of
Compassion and Personal Fulfillment

WILLIAM BLOOM

QUEST

BOOKS

Theosophical Publishing House
Wheaton, Illinois * Chennai, India

First Quest Edition 2012

First published in the United Kingdom by Piatkus, an imprint of Little, Brown Book Group

Quest Books
Theosophical Publishing House
PO Box 270
Wheaton, IL 60187-0270
www.questbooks.net

Library of Congress Cataloging-in-Publication Data

Bloom, William
[Power of modern spirituality]
The power of the new spirituality: how to live a life of compassion and personal fulfillment/William Bloom.—1st. Quest ed.
     p.   cm.
Includes bibliographical references and index.
Originally published under title: Power of modern spirituality: how to live a life of compassion and personal fulfilment. London: Piatkus, 2011.
ISBN 978-0-8356-0906-7
1. Spirituality.   2. Spiritual life.   I. Title.
BL624.B565 2012
204—dc23   2012012424

5 4 3 2 1 * 12 13 14 15 16

Printed in the United States of America

For Sophie

Contents

Preface   ix
Acknowledgments   xi

Introduction: The New Spirituality   1

Part One: Connection
1. Your Connection with the Wonder and Energy of Life   33
2. Deepening Your Experience   53

Part Two: Reflection
3. Awakening and Self-Management   87
4. The Challenges of Spiritual Growth   119

Part Three: Service
5. Being True to Your Highest Values   159
6. Presence, Prayer, and Healing   181

Conclusion: The Extra Dimension   207

Appendix A: Spiritual Companions' Guidelines   219
Appendix B: Spiritual Emergency—Care and First Aid   223
Appendix C: Next Steps and More Resources   227
Notes   231
Glossary   239
Recommended Reading   241
Index   247

Preface

✳

It is March 2011, and in front of me is the questionnaire for the UK Census. I am looking particularly at the section entitled "What Is Your Religion?" I can tick "No Religion," "Christian," "Buddhist," "Hindu," "Jewish," "Muslim," "Sikh." Or I can write something in the seventeen spaces for individual letters allocated to "Any other religion."

I might meet a similar question in a hospital form or a job application. Well, what *is* my religion? Part of me would like to tick all the boxes and then write something like "spiritual but not religious" or "I respect the essence of all spiritual traditions," but those are all longer than the seventeen spaces allowed me. Personally, I like the word *holistic* in this context, but that may not be the right word for you. A friend of mine likes the word *universalist*. Other friends and colleagues say that the essence of modern spirituality is its diversity, so it is wrong anyway to try to name it in one box or one word.

But one thing is certain. Whatever it is called, a new spirituality is emerging, and if you have any instinct for or curiosity about this fresh approach, then this book is, I hope, for you. My purpose here is to describe the new spirituality's major features and how it can be practiced in daily life.

Over the decades, I have taught and worked with many open-minded and open-hearted people from education and the caring professions, so it is my intention that this book serve too as a useful text for people who for professional reasons need to understand spirituality in a modern context. This warmly includes clergy and members of traditional faiths, as well as secularists and those of a pagan disposition.

But, whether you are professionally interested or inquiring for personal reasons, my heartfelt hope is that you find the content of this book as inspiring and useful as I have found the research and exploration for it.

William Bloom

Glastonbury, 2011

Acknowledgments

✳

In the first place I must express appreciation and gratitude to all my colleagues and students who have supported and stimulated me. I am deeply grateful especially to my companions and close friends in the Spiritual Companions project, the Open Mystery School, and the Foundation for Holistic Spirituality. There are too many of you to name, but you know who you are, and I truly appreciate your affection, forbearance, and inspiration.

This book is also the result of a long process of writing and research, and its ideas were first developed in my *First Steps* and then *Soulution: The Holistic Manifesto*. Clarifying my thoughts was also supported by the regular articles I wrote in *Cygnus* magazine. I owe thanks to all those supportive editors and publishers. My agent, Liz Puttick, has also been a source of consistent encouragement.

The Power of the New Spirituality was also preceded by a privately circulated course book for the Spiritual Companions courses. I thank my students and colleagues for their engagement and helpful feedback.

In the editing, improving, and rewriting of this book, my editors at Piatkus, Claudia Dyer and Gill Bailey, were wonderfully generous, insightful, and intelligent. I am very grateful to them. Also thanks go to Andrew John for his finishing editorial touches.

The landscape, spirits, and people of Glastonbury—a unique multifaith culture—where I live, have also provided a congruent and enjoyable environment for this work. Beyond my neighborhood, I have a network of good friends working in similar terrain whose solidarity is always there. And, most importantly, I live in a home where my writing is appreciated and affectionately supported.

I feel blessed and grateful.

THE NEW SPIRITUALITY

✷

In January 2009 a scholarly paper in *Psychological Bulletin* included a provocative claim that religious believers manage better in life. Entitled "Religion, Self-Regulation, and Self-Control," it analyzed eight decades of rigorous research and concluded that believers performed better, had better health and greater happiness, and lived longer than nonbelievers.

The authors were academics and not aligned with any particular faith. They had no interest in persuading people to adopt one religion or another. Their analysis was a dispassionate assessment based on thorough research. Their paper ended by suggesting possible explanations for why religion seems to work so successfully, such as self-control and effective goal setting, but the authors were honest about the fact that they did not really understand their conclusions and that further research was needed.[1]

This is tantalizing, isn't it? Eight decades of research. Believers perform better, have better health, and live longer. But this rigorously researched paper self-confessedly had no clarity about why this is so. There is a further tantalization, too, which creates an immediate tension. Here we have something that can help us enhance our lives. Thank you. Yes, please: of *course* we would love to manage our lives better, be happier, and live longer.

But we have this challenge, which is that it all comes tangled up with religion. Hmm. This is delicate. Thank you, but no, thank you.

Introduction

We want the benefits of religion and spirituality, but we do not necessarily want to buy into a set of beliefs, get into a faith box, or join an organized group.

So there is something useful and wonderful here, but we do not know what it is—and, even if we did know what it is, it might entangle us in stuff that is not quite so wonderful.

This is an intriguing puzzle and the purpose of this book is to solve it. Can we perform an alchemical act and extract the golden essence? Can we have the benefits without getting caught up in the deficits? I believe this is possible. We can indeed extract what is valuable in spirituality in a way that is accessible and understandable to people of all and no faiths. We can make it clear and practical, inspiring and meaningful, of profound benefit to ourselves and those around us. In order to do this, however, we need to perceive and appreciate what lies at the very heart of religion, and separate its essence from its form, discerning the important difference between organized institutional beliefs and spiritual experience.

The real task, therefore, is to understand what the many forms of personal spirituality have in common, regardless of their culture and circumstances. To express it more provocatively, suppose, for example, we were able to meet Jesus or Buddha in person, without all the superstructure of the beliefs and organizations that later ensued. What would be the similarities in their personal spirituality? Or on a lesser scale, what might be the spiritual common ground held by Saint Francis of Assisi and Nelson Mandela and the Burmese opposition leader Aung San Suu Kyi?

This book is about discerning that spiritual essence, clarifying it, and making it practically accessible and doable by all of us.

THE BENEFITS OF SPIRITUALITY

The benefits of religion and spirituality are, as the scholarly paper suggested, worthwhile: "Believers perform better, have better health, greater happiness, and live longer." In fact, there are many boons to spirituality that I want to list for you, but I hesitate.

I hesitate because I do not want to be accused of spiritual materialism. I do not want to commoditize spirituality and turn it into just another twenty-first-century self-help product or app that promises to make you feel better. I am not comfortable with that kind of spirituality. This week, I offer you a new meditation practice. Next week, it will be a new recipe or trainers or golf clubs or saints' bones. This book is not in that kind of business. It is in the business of developing our hearts, deepening and expanding our awareness, and building a just, creative, and benevolent world.

Yet, Lord knows, it is understandable why people—you and I—would want a quick fix. Especially today, caught in streams of never-ending information, relentless change, and stimulation, life continuously challenges us, and it would be a blessing if there were easy relief. But there are already many sources of temporary relief: a good meal, friends, shopping, a holiday, sport, and arts. Unfortunately, the respite they bring us does not last long, and surely we deserve better than just the occasional oasis of relaxation and contentment. Spirituality promises something deeper and more enduring.

How about a life that is filled with meaning and purpose, and a deep rumbling excitement at the sheer exhilaration of existence and your being part of it? How about a sense of personal integrity and a joy that passes all understanding? How about a form of personal development that is the best and most interesting process in the world? How about being a presence that reassures and brings healing?

Spirituality can bring us:

- connection with the wonder and energy of all life;

- values and the fuel to be good, do good, and serve others;

- development of heart, compassion, and consciousness;

- a mindful, solid, and inspiring strength to carry us through good and bad times;

- a sense of meaning, personal integrity, and purpose independent of material success and the opinion of others;

- an embedded sense of well-being to support physical and mental health; and

- a deep enjoyment of life that is also fully present to its challenges and suffering.

THREE GOLDEN KEYS

But naming all those positive assets still leaves us with the big question. We know what the results look like, but how do we actually achieve them?

In one of my classes on the new spirituality I asked the students, "What is spirituality for you?" Their answers included less materialism; compassion; consciousness; self-awareness; love; quest; death of self; trust; discernment; openheartedness; wholeness and full connection with God; self-respect; care and healing; true purpose; peace; harmony; simplicity; letting go; understanding; freedom; wisdom.

These are all inspiring things, but, again, the issue is, how do we actually achieve them? What do we actually have to do? What is the activity and practice? There is a difference between listening to music and making music, between eating and cooking, between being a spectator and being engaged. What we are focusing on here is the engagement and activity.

In this book I suggest that if we look carefully at spirituality in all its many forms, we will find three key practices, three golden keys, that sit at the heart of all of them. Moreover, I suggest that these three practices were not invented by spiritual teachers in order to help us, but are innate and part of us just because we are human.

Whether you know it or not, you do spirituality just because you are alive.

My major purpose in this book is to support you in being aware of what you already do naturally and instinctively. I then want to give you further support so that you have the understanding and skills to deepen and fully integrate your spirituality.

So what are these three key practices? Let me answer by posing three questions to you:

- In what kind of circumstances do you most easily connect with the wonder and energy of nature and all existence, and feel your heart touched and your consciousness awakened?

- When is it easiest for you to retreat from activity, pause, and reflect on your life, so as to manage your life and next steps?

- What are your highest values, and how do you express them as a form of service for the community of life?

Don't you do all of these already in some way?

Connection: sometimes, surely, your heart is touched and you connect with the wonder and energy of life.

Reflection: sometimes, already, you pause and reflect on your life and actions, and ponder how to change and improve.

Service: and sometimes, of course, you have a clear sense of what is right and what is wrong, and you act so as to do good for others.

There you have them—three key behaviors at the heart of spirituality and to be found in all traditions and approaches. One of the pleasures of my life is those moments when students or colleagues realize they are already doing what they think they have to learn: "Ah, I'm doing it already! I'm already connecting with the wonder and energy of life. I know when my heart is touched and I can sense my compassion arising and my mood softening." "Yes, I often pause and look at my life. The more honest I am, the better. This builds my kindness and my ability to care." "I know my values and I live by them. I honor compassion, freedom, and social justice."

Connection. Reflection. Service. The flow and structure of this book is centered on these three key practices, clarifying them, making them more conscious, and showing you how to explore and strengthen them.

But let me be clear. All of this is to be developed and lived by you according to your own unique and authentic understanding. If there is one thing I have had to learn and celebrate about our spirituality, it is that everyone is an independent and sovereign individual. Just as you choose your friends, choose your food, your clothes, or your career, so you also may freely choose and create your own spirituality. Your spirituality is your creation. And my purpose here is to support and encourage your authentic spirituality and avoid boxes of belief, expectation, or conformity.

CENTERING AND KIND WATCHFULNESS

What you will find in this book is the distillation of forty years of personal practice and thirty years of teaching and researching, exploring what actually works for people. It has all been tried and tested over years, so that everything in it can be done as part of your normal and regular life. Because I work with students and colleagues from many different backgrounds and cultures, I am also confident that this approach is universally supportive, regardless of your belief system.

There is nothing here that will require spiritual extremism from you. There is no need for you to copy the fifth-century Saint Symeon the Stylite, who lived on top of a column in northern Syria for thirty-nine years in order to develop his holiness. Nor that you emulate the eleventh-century Tibetan yogi Milarepa, who lived in seclusion, eating only nettles until he turned completely green.

I am very realistic about the fact that most of us work and pay bills, have relationships and family, queue up at the supermarket, have mortgages and careers, and wrestle with the challenges and pleasures of the human condition.

I am also a passionate advocate of deep democracy and believe in the absolute spiritual equality of all people—no castes, no elites, no privileges or special ordinations. As a writer and teacher, therefore, I am dedicated to exploring and explaining the essence of spiritual experience and spiritual development in a language that is transparent and speaks to everyone.

At the same time, having affirmed our democratic and equal relationship, I believe the usefulness of someone like me is that I can save you unnecessary time and effort. I am not going to abandon you to experimentation and having to reinvent the wheel. In particular, I can remind you of the core skills that are absolutely necessary for those wanting to manage their own development on the spiritual path.

This practice is like painting, music, or any craft. You can be as eccentric and as unique as you like, but nevertheless you need to understand your materials and tools. In this respect, for example, you can be as individualistic as you like in your spirituality, but, like all of us, you do need to know how to press your pause button, center into your heart, and switch on an attitude of kind watchfulness. No matter what kind of spirituality we practice, we all need those basic skills, or else we flounder.

So, while I will encourage you throughout the book to maintain your individuality, I will also simultaneously be explaining these essential basic skills and prompting you to use them. I will lay all of this out as explicitly and as clearly as I possibly can, so that you can develop your spiritual practice in the same way as you might diligently attend to any other part of your life. And I really want this approach to support you, whatever your temperament.

Again, one of my pleasures is when people recognize that they are already utilizing these skills: "Yes, I *know* how to pause, detach, and be kindly watchful"; "So being centered and grounded is when I'm not running around like a headless chicken and can stand there, calm in the midst of chaos. OK, I've done that"; "So *that's* what's happening when I sigh and yield to the sheer beauty of being alive. I can feel my connection with the wonder and energy."

MY STORY

In the next section we will explore more fully the unique historical circumstances out of which the new spirituality is born, but before that it is right and appropriate that you know about my own background and history, and how I developed what is presented in this book.

It is always good for people to know and understand the background and character of teachers or experts, because these factors will certainly influence their teaching. At the same time, this book is about you and your spirituality, so, if you choose to jump this biographical section about me and go straight into the next section, you will miss nothing that builds the knowledge of this book, and I will happily meet you there.

Yes, I am experienced in spirituality, with many books written or edited on the subject, courses taught, and projects directed. Yes, my history includes a two-year retreat and a daily meditation practice over forty years. And, yes, I have been a spokesperson over many years for the new spirituality in the media and conferences. But strip away the activities and products, and there I am, on my own, like all of us, wrestling with myself, struggling to become more loving, more connected, and more conscious.

I am the classic example of a man teaching what I want and need to learn.

I was brought up in central London. My parents were intellectual humanistic agnostics, hostile to religion, my father from a Jewish and my mother from a Lutheran background. As a child, like many children, I could easily feel the wonder of nature and the cosmos. I looked at the blue of the sky and wondered whether it was the blue of God's eye. I wondered, too, why people went to temple or church, rather than enjoying the awesome dome of the heavens. At the same time, at nursery, my heart was opened and my compassion touched when I saw an awkward child being bullied. I instinctively knew that this was wrong and she needed care.

Alongside my occasional insightfulness and kindness, I was also rebellious, judgmental, and arrogant. Decades on, I still have these two traits inside me—kindness and rebellion—but they are today mediated by a kind watchfulness that was developed first of all by three years of psychoanalysis in my twenties, then by a doctorate in psychology and decades of daily practice in meditation.

My childhood sense of life's magic was reinforced in 1960s' London, where I was lucky enough as a teenager to be pollinated by flower power with its ethos of love, its embrace of Eastern and tribal spiritualities, and its adventurous exploration of anything—yoga, meditation, psychotherapy, psychotropic substances, chanting, dance—that expanded consciousness. This lifestyle, however, developed into a serious interest, and I began to study religion and spirituality in earnest, particularly fascinated by the similarities of mystic Christianity, Jewish Kabala, the Sufi tradition of Islam, Zen Buddhism, and Tibetan shamanism. At the same time my career as an author and publisher, although successful, did not give me satisfaction, so I committed fully to spiritual inquiry and took a two-year self-directed retreat in the High Atlas Mountains of southern Morocco to study, reflect, pray, meditate, and become closer to nature.

After I returned to London I never expected or planned to be a teacher of spirituality, but started to do it informally, mainly sharing meditation and centering strategies in my early thirties. I then cofounded and for ten years codirected the Alternatives lecture and workshop program in St. James's Church, Piccadilly, London, a program that became the UK's leading platform of the new spirituality. During that decade I hosted hundreds of the world's best-known authors and teachers in the field of spirituality. If I wanted to learn about a particular tradition or understand a practice, I was in a position to invite the experts to London and experience their approach.

I estimate that I must have personally experienced more than five hundred different approaches to spiritual and personal development. This may seem overwhelming to some readers, but I was an enthusiast. Someone who loves cars or literature or cuisine will also explore widely. It was a wonderful education.

At the same time, following on from my three years of psychoanalysis, I investigated and benefited from the wide variety of therapies now available, including spiritual healing, talk therapy, cocounseling, gestalt, bodywork, breath work, transpersonal psychotherapy, hypnotherapy, sweat lodges, and more. I mention all of these not as an indication of my neediness, but to illustrate that I have tried the best I can, as part of my professional development and due diligence, to get as full a picture as possible of what is available and useful. These many strategies have also hugely supported my growth. In particular they helped to integrate my buzzing mind down into my body, feelings, and emotions; or, to put it in more spiritual language, they helped my soul land in the temple of my body.

Alongside my own books and articles, I have edited or coedited four anthologies and encyclopedias of the new spirituality, which have helped, too, to keep me fully abreast of our modern diversity.[2] I love editing books, devising educational programs, and providing platforms for spiritual variety to be enjoyed.

In the midst of this wonderful variety, I also had to clarify my thinking about the new spirituality and bring some coherence to it, because I was regularly called upon to represent it at seminars and conferences, where I often met intelligent criticism, skepticism, and sometimes hostility. I wear as a badge of honor being the only speaker to be booed at the United Nations 1998 Oslo Conference on Freedom of Belief when I represented a new approach to spirituality. A group of clergy objected to my suggestion that everyone, just by being alive, is connected to the wonder and energy of existence. In their opinion, God alone decided, through grace, who is and who is not spiritual.

I also experienced many confrontations when I represented the new spirituality to the media, especially on BBC Radio 4 talk programs such as *Sunday* and *The Moral Maze*. To begin with, I experienced embarrassment and disempowerment because I was inarticulate and could not effectively represent this new movement. Today, after exploring and clarifying the ideas presented in this book, I am ready and available for rigorous debate. I am, for example, very active in a campaign suggesting that when you encounter forms and questionnaires, perhaps in a hospital, that ask "What Is Your Religion?" you might use the word *holistic*—being shorthand for an openhearted approach that respects the essence of all spiritual approaches (see the glossary for many terms that appear in this book).

In parallel with all this, over the last twenty-five years I have developed a series of trainings, workshops, and courses in the new spirituality, exploring the essence of spirituality when it is stripped bare of its religious beliefs, symbols, mythologies, and metaphors. Of particular relevance is a project I started in the 1990s called the Open Mystery School, which then developed into the Spiritual Companions project, a training in a multifaith and holistic approach to spirituality and pastoral care. These two programs were crucial in clarifying the concepts and practices presented in this book as we explored, for example, what lies at the heart of worship or ceremony or meditation or the creation of sacred space, when the surrounding beliefs are dissolved. These courses attracted many feisty and independent-minded students and colleagues, many of whom were also educators and professional carers. They were perfect companions, ensuring that the courses were practical, clear, and ethical.

Out of these explorations emerged a course book, which has been completely rewritten and transformed into the book you are now reading, and also a set of guidelines, called the Spiritual Companions Guidelines, which you will find in Appendix A.

One of the most important insights that emerged out of all this educational and spiritual research was the realization that, regardless of our level of experience, we all need to be doing the same things. It might seem, for example, because I have been meditating and teaching spirituality for decades, that I should be practicing differently from people who have just started consciously walking their spiritual paths. But, whether we are apparently experienced or apparently beginners, the essence of spiritual work is always the same: love and compassion, consciousness and awareness, values and service.

As you read this book, therefore, I hope you experience a sense of equality, companionship, and collegiality.

NEW OPPORTUNITIES IN A CHANGING WORLD

For some people, I know, it is provocative even to claim there is such a thing as a modern or new spirituality. They would say that spirituality has always been the same and always will be. And I reply that is partly true, but there have been such startling changes in our culture, society, and understanding of life that it really is a new situation. Historically, all the world religions emerged out of and reflected the societies and cultures of their times. None of those cultures resemble today's world.

In the remainder of this chapter, I want to describe clearly the circumstances that have birthed the new spirituality and influenced it. I also want to look at some of the challenges it can bring to us, such as confusion and a lack of clarity when we are faced with so many choices.

Skeptics may assume that, because the new spirituality is a child of the modern world, it is necessarily tainted by all the materialism and noise. But this is untrue. The new spirituality is essentially a child of the many good things about modernity, many of which we may take for granted. We need to be clear about the social circumstances out of which all the traditional faiths arose and how different they are from today. Let your imagination go back two thousand years and fully engage with what it was like. Illiterate. Uneducated. Unrepresented. No democracy. Little travel. Slavery. Sexism. Average age, thirty-five. Most children died in infancy or before the age of five. Uncertainty about food and survival. No media.

Imagine, then, the power and charisma of those who had education, an aura of confidence, and a gift for oratory or storytelling. And then look at today's circumstances, at least for almost half the world's population, and allow yourself to imagine what kind of spirituality you might expect to arise from this radically new environment.

Literacy and education are basic human rights. You are a free person in a democratized society, and no one tells you what to do or believe. You are now independently knowledge-rich and participate in a world of free-flowing information. In your hands, in a smart phone or some other gizmo, you have a digital world of knowledge, opinions, and messages. Fed and housed, you have time for more than just survival.

These are spectacularly different circumstances from the cultural milieux out of which Judaism, Hinduism, Buddhism, Christianity, and Islam emerged.

THE GLOBAL VILLAGE OF FREE-FLOWING INFORMATION

This free flow of information to an educated mass population is crucial. We have come a long way from men chiseling messages on stone or painstakingly copying manuscripts for a literate elite. With a solar-powered tablet, any one of us anywhere has access to the world of almost all knowledge, certainly to all the world's sacred scriptures, ceremonies, and strategies that were previously separated by geography, secrecy, and language.

In schools today, children learn about the beliefs and rites of all the world's religions. In healthcare and well-being, you may be using strategies from spiritual practices such as yoga, martial arts, or meditation that were previously unknown in the West, and even in the East were restricted to an expert elite of specialists. Indigenous spiritualities and shamanic traditions from tribal peoples all over the world are also now accessible.

A few centuries ago dominant opinion would almost always come from high representatives of the local church, temple, or mosque, usually in alliance with the dominant political force, monarch, or emperor. Today, the major faiths have innumerable competitors commenting on the meaning of life, from the worlds of psychology, feminism, sociology, philosophy, and science, as well as many journalists and freelance commentators. Anyone with a media profile can comment on the big questions of life, and phone-ins and digital chat rooms give us all the opportunity to participate.

Immediately you can see how this widespread access to diverse ideas is bound to change the form of religion. Historically, the world's great religions, East and West, tended to be centered on the single teaching of a single person, with a hierarchy of monks, priests, and scholars maintaining and developing the lore.

In the contemporary situation, on the other hand, you are a free agent able to explore a wide variety of different approaches. These new cultural dynamics encourage you in individual spiritual self-management, supported by diverse knowledge and resources. This is publicly exemplified in the books and television documentaries of those, some of them clergy, who pursue their spiritual path through exploring different faiths.[3] You may have seen the adventurous Anglican vicar Peter Owen Jones pursuing his spiritual inquiry in the British television program *Extreme Pilgrim*, spending time with holy men in China, India, and Egypt.[4] Or the journalist Elizabeth Gilbert conducting her spiritual development through various disciplines in *Eat, Pray, Love*.[5]

Introduction

SELF-DETERMINATION AND DIVERSITY

And there is more. The last two centuries have also seen a new under-standing of what it means to be human. At its most profound, this perspective asserts that we are all evolving, developmental beings, always in the process of change and growth. We are not just animals or slaves or sinners or victims of karma, chained to our social station of caste and class. It is a basic human right that we be educated and able to develop and fulfill our potential.

You therefore have the freedom to make your own crucial deci-sions about your life. Best practice in medicine, for example, is about empowering you to self-manage your own health and well-being, using the medical profession as a wise partner rather than a dominant authority. You research your own illness, learn about the options, and then discuss the best way forward with your doctor.

You can see this too in the way that news and editorial are no longer monopolized by an elite of professional media commentators, but are balanced by the information emerging from diverse social networks and new-media streams. At any time you want, you can feed news and commentary into the media through the blogosphere and social networking, and also directly to producers and editors.

Education is also changing. Walk into most classrooms today and you will find small groups of children working together around tables instead of sitting in regimented rows receiving knowledge from an expert. Even large corporations, previously models of top-down hierarchical authority, are evolving into networks of executives com-municating as equals as they face shared goals and challenges.

All of this is the learning and communications culture of the new global village. Information flows feely, and people are involved in self-managed decision making about their lives and futures—all people, not just an educated or power-based elite.

Belief, faith, religion, and spirituality are not separate from this new environment. Brought up in these circumstances, you would naturally want to create and build your own spirituality and beliefs, in the same way as you have freedom in the rest of your life. The new spirituality directly reflects this liberated individuality taking place within a new world of information and knowledge.

Of course, all of this is bound to be challenging for those who are instinctive conservatives and have previously been comfortable respecting fixed and traditional hierarchy and authority. To anyone whose main allegiance is to a particular tradition, this new situation may understandably cause concerns, but more than a hundred years ago the Hindu teacher Swami Vivekananda addressed them. When the first World Parliament of Religions was held in Chicago in 1893, he told the story of a frog who lived in a well. This frog then met another frog, who lived in the ocean. The frog from the small well refused to believe there was anything more special than his well. Vivekananda suggested that traditional religions were sometimes like that frog in the well. They needed to appreciate the greater ocean.

This new democracy, self-determination, and variety of choices do not mean that we reject wise and experienced help. It just means that we are liberated from deference, into partnership. We are not children, and it was never psychologically healthy to be infantilized by priests, gurus, institutions, or belief systems.

There is also a wonderful silver lining to this multifaith awareness, especially when children learn about other people's religions and beliefs, which thankfully happens today in most multicultural education around the world. Previously, people were suspicious of and hostile to other spiritual approaches just because they were strange and new, but this new education engenders familiarity and mutual respect. This approach is, for example, clearly supported by UNESCO, which asserts that an understanding of diverse cultures and religions is a core element of sustainable education.[6] Equally, in countries such as France and the United States where there is a constitutional separation between state and religion, there is nevertheless also a clear appreciation of the need to learn about the world's faiths.

Introduction

One of the keynotes of a modern society is its relaxed and appreciative attitude toward diverse cultures and beliefs and its respect for individual choices. All of this is a blessing to be cherished as we remember those fundamentalist cultures where spiritual and other freedoms are still repressed.

THE ACCUSATION OF NO VALUES

But, with all this freedom, individualism, and diversity, the new spirituality can also look shallow and ephemeral, like a supermarket with shiny options from all over the world that seekers, like magpies, can acquire to decorate their nests. A bit of Dalai Lama here. Some Celtic Christianity there. Some Kabbala on the wrist. Indeed, at its worst, you can find strategies claiming to be "spiritual" that overtly promise financial wealth and material success, completely disdaining ideas of compassion and consciousness. So it is not surprising that some people look at all the contemporary therapies, strategies, and spiritual paths on offer and despair at their apparent selfishness.

It was not pleasant for me, for example, when one of my heroes, Archbishop Trevor Huddleston, consistently ignored me when I worked in the rectory of St. James's Church, Piccadilly, where he lived for a while in the small top-floor apartment. He was one of the most politically engaged and courageous of Anglican priests, a founder of the antiapartheid movement and a force for good. I kept passing him on the stairs of the rectory, and I always greeted him politely, but he would turn his eyes away or grunt.

Finally one day, after two years of this strange behavior, I slightly obstructed his passage on the stairs so that he had to look me in the eyes. This wiry and passionate man gave me a very quick and punching lecture before moving past me. "You and your people have no historical foundation," he accused. "No heritage of ethics and values. No philosophical roots. You have no sense of your context and, therefore, nothing useful to say about real-world injustices and morality."

I suddenly understood his attitude toward me. He knew I had cofounded and was directing the Alternatives Programme in the church and he did not like what he saw. He, like many others looking at this new approach to spirituality, perceived it to be a child of the modern capitalist and consumer-driven world, a shallow set of options for self-centered people seeking personal happiness and material success, with no awareness of social reality and no values. Me, me, me. My health. My fulfillment. My happiness.

All the great religious teachers and traditions speak clearly about the moral imperative to do good, but where does the new spirituality stand? It has all this wonderful diversity, but where are its values and its moral guidelines?

I have met this criticism many times and was particularly struck by it when a journalist one day bluntly said to me, echoing precisely what Archbishop Huddleston had said, "Your lot appear to have no values. And nobody will take you seriously until you do."

POWERFUL SHARED VALUES

The accusation that the new spirituality has no values is understandable, because they are rarely articulated, but it is untrue. Any suggestion that it ignores classical ethical teachings and has no traditional roots is also wrong. Forgive me here if I begin to sound too strident, but I must admit to a frustration with the casual assumption about the lack of ethics and no ethos of service. It is a flip criticism that deserves robust refutation.

When people accuse the new spirituality of ignoring or even dumbing down traditional values, they are missing what, in fact, is one of the great strengths of a new approach. Instead of seeing all the different religions as being in moral conflict with each other, the new spirituality welcomes and highlights the ethical similarities. The new spirituality absolutely embraces, honors, and supports the core ethics and morality of all the world's religions and great philosophies. Religion by religion, philosophy by philosophy, these values are similar. Be charitable. Look after each other. Do not kill. Do not steal. Do not rape. Do not harm. Do unto others as you would have them do unto you. The new spirituality supports these core values.

It is inspiring to see the same messages promoting love and justice in all the world's faiths. A multifaith approach does not dilute morality. It strengthens values because we can see they are universal and not just the preserve of one belief system. It holistically includes and combines core ethics, reinforcing, not weakening, them. It also recognizes how these universal values are also expressed in important secular declarations such as the United Nations Declaration of Human Rights, which was adopted by the United Nations in 1948 after the Second World War and represented the first global expression of rights to which all human beings are inherently entitled, and also the Earth Charter, the influential statement on sustainability published in June 2000.[7]

However, because of those consistent criticisms, I developed my own personal-values statement for the new spirituality, and I also helped to develop a more general statement. This is the essence of my own statement:

> The new spirituality, with which I am aligned, absolutely embraces, respects, and supports the core ethics and morality of all the world's religions and great philosophies. Instead of seeing them as being in competition, it plaits them together to make an ethical statement that is even stronger because of their combined reinforcement.
>
> Moreover, the new spirituality introduces three other core values—those of the *green movement*, that we love, respect, and care for all of the natural world; those of *developmental psychology*, that we respect, care for, and give affection to all human beings; and the *metaphysical* value that we take responsibility for the atmosphere and vibrations we radiate.

I also participated in the creation of a more general statement for the nonprofit foundation for which I work. To achieve this we looked at the world's best-known and most-respected ethical statements, from the Ten Commandments, through the United Nations Declaration on Human Rights, the Earth Charter, and Harvard Business School's code of ethics, to the code of conduct of the National Federation of Spiritual Healers. We then made a database of all the key words and terms in those statements, counted up which words and concepts appeared the most frequently, and then formed them into a single statement, which appears below.

The statement below may not be perfect, but it points in the right direction, and the process of creating it was a good consciousness-raising exercise for all involved.

HOLISTIC-VALUES STATEMENT

The values named here are high ideals and are always work in progress. They are presented in no particular order of priority.

Inclusion and Respect
I welcome diversity of belief, faith, ethnicity, gender, sexual orientation, intellect, ability, and age—and value the unique contribution of every individual.

Environment
I recognize the sacred interdependence of all life and behave so as to protect the health and sustainability of our natural environment now and for future generations.

Spirituality
I recognize spirituality to be a normal and healthy part of daily life, as people experience the wonder of nature and all creation;

---

and I celebrate the many paths that explore this wonder and its meaning.

Relationships

At home, at work, and in my community, I am committed to respectful, loving and positive relationships.

Lifestyle

I maintain a lifestyle and gain my income in ways that benefit and do no harm.

Global and Local Citizenship

I actively engage to build community, alleviate injustice, and relieve suffering; and deplore any situation that limits the rights, development, and fulfillment of any being.

Self-Responsibility

I am actively committed to managing my own health and development; and I value life as an ongoing process of learning.

But these words are not your words, and I strongly recommend that, both on your own and perhaps in any group you are a part of, you develop your own statement. We will return to this important subject later.

TRADITIONAL, GREEN, PSYCHOLOGICAL, AND METAPHYSICAL VALUES

More than that, the new spirituality brings other important agendas to the table, as we saw in the preceding section: the values of the environmental movement, of developmental psychology (the study of psychological development along the lifespan), and of metaphysics (the study of subtle energies and invisible dimensions).

This focus on green issues comes partly from the ecological crisis. Nearly all of us have now woken up and become aware that sustainability is a crucial issue for the healthy survival of humanity and the natural world. Environmental awareness is now both high on the agenda of central government and a core part of the school curriculum. But there is a more important spiritual source for green values, which derives from pagan, tribal, and shamanic cultures.

At the heart of all these native teachings is a close and empathic relationship with nature and an appreciation that everything—every blade of grass, every rock, every creature—is alive and sacred. The natural world is our family, and we have a kinship with all living beings. The new spirituality welcomes and learns from these previously repressed, ignored, or unknown traditions.

The new spirituality also includes the core insights of developmental psychology, which began to emerge in the late decades of the nineteenth century with a more humane understanding of children's education and growth. One of those core insights is that children and adults develop fully only if they receive love and care. We all need food, shelter, education, and safety. But just as crucial is emotional care and warmth, without which people wither and, at worst, become dangers to themselves and others.

If we are to grow a peaceful and harmonious human society, we have to treat each other with emotional and psychological realism. Heartrending research has been done on children abandoned in orphanages, who receive little human stimulation or affection and whose brains and nervous systems do not develop properly.[8] For the new spirituality, psychological literacy, kindness, and emotional care are moral imperatives. Without this care, we are literally less than human.

Finally, and I will discuss this in detail later, the new spirituality also brings in an ethical awareness that will seem strange to some and completely obvious to others—that we need to take responsibility for the subtle vibrations and mood that we radiate into our lives. This is a normal concept in shamanic traditions and also in those spiritualities that take seriously the effects of spiritual healing, prayer, and the influence of someone's presence.

At the biological level, a dog can smell when someone is tense or radiating aggression. The adrenaline sours the aroma of your perspiration. At a more subtle level, as with electric eels, metaphysics suggests that we emit an electromagnetic aura that affects other people. Anyone who is naturally empathic or aware of atmospheres can sense when someone is in a bad or a good mood—and this is not just because of their body language. Blind people attest to this often, and you yourself may often have experienced knowing the mood of people who come into your home or close to you before you physically see them.

If you happen to be thick skinned and skeptical about this, then I suggest you take notice of the millions of others who are not so well insulated and do sense the atmosphere of when someone is in a foul or a benevolent mood. It affects people, and it can have a disastrous bullying influence on children and those weaker than oneself.

So the new spirituality is also clear about this metaphysical ethos: monitor and manage your mood, so that you radiate a benevolent presence and not a bullying and polluting ambience.

You can see, then, I hope, that the new spirituality has a powerful code of ethics, combining the core values of the world faiths with the moral imperatives of green awareness and psychological care, and a very direct call to take responsibility for the mood you radiate into the world around you. Now, to put all this into practice is a high calling, and we may never get it perfect, but we are all in the process of getting there.

The Values of the New Spirituality

Traditional values of the world's religious and secular traditions—charity, justice, compassion, "do unto others as you would have done unto you"

+ **green values**—protect and care for the natural world

+ **psychological/emotional values**—give love, respect, and affection

+ **presence**—radiate benevolence, not pollution

= **values of the new spirituality**

HIDING OUR BELIEFS IN THE CLOSET

It took me several years of often-uncomfortable confrontation to achieve some clarity about the values of the new spirituality, summed up as an equation above. It needed conversation and debate.

But spirituality, especially personal spirituality, is often not considered a normal topic for conversation. People do not usually chat about it in the way they might talk about their health or sport or fashion. This reticence is paradoxical, because spirituality is explicitly high on the agenda in, for example, education and healthcare. The first paragraphs of the England and Wales Education Act of 2002 legislate for "a balanced and broadly based curriculum which promotes the spiritual, moral, cultural, mental and physical development of children and of society." Equally the National Health Service has an explicit call for spirituality to be included in best practice, and, in a poll of British nurses taken in 2010, 80 percent felt that spirituality needed to be included in their education.[9]

There is also a clear intellectual understanding that spirituality is different from religion and a growing general sense of its value in a form that is disengaged from traditional faith. In his book *Spiritual But Not Religious*, Robert Fuller shows that a fifth of all Americans would sign up for that precise tag "spiritual but not religious."[10] And the ongoing research of the World Values Survey indicates that in modern societies across the world where people are well educated, fed, and housed, up to 70 percent of the population have moved on from strict alliance with a single religion to a more open and generalized spirituality.[11]

But, even with this public acknowledgement of spirituality, people are shy to talk about it. I have one friend who for many years was the successful and innovating chief executive of an international company and kept completely silent about his spirituality throughout that whole period. He once wrote to me, "I feel I let you down and all the people like you by being a 'closet' spirit! And had I been braver and more open—and people had seen that my progress was because of my spirituality rather than despite it, then I think other people would have come forward and done the same."

Of course, there are also people who may be very public about their spirituality, often film, sports, and music stars, but these are people who are happy anyway to be in the public eye. For people of a more modest or cautious disposition, it is not that easy to communicate about one's spirituality. It can be very isolating and also have negative consequences. This was the situation for Nigel, my codirector in the Foundation for Holistic Spirituality. For many years he was a high-flying project manager in an international business consultancy, and, when his interest in spirituality began to develop, he found he had no appropriate language so that he could talk with his wife and colleagues about it.

When we first started working together, he once said to me, "It would have been so much easier for me if spirituality were normal. Why can't spirituality just be a normal part of everyday life and conversation?" In one form or another I have heard his request many times, as people from many different walks of life share with me that they keep quiet about their spirituality.

I understand Nigel's experience only too well, for I remember, when I was working in education, how I too was shy about my spirituality, exactly like a gay man being wary of coming out of the closet. There I was, well educated, several books published, a doctorate, some status. But I was nevertheless withholding my true thoughts and beliefs. I kept them private because, if and when I opened up about my spirituality, I was concerned that I would be either misunderstood or mocked.

LEARNING TO TALK ABOUT SPIRITUALITY

So I confess to another personal passion here. I do not want people to feel isolated in their spirituality, unable to talk openly about it. I want spirituality to be as normal a topic for conversation as cooking or health or sport. I am not talking about standing on a soapbox, seeking converts, or demanding attention. I am just talking about normal conversations and interactions in which we develop mutual understanding.

How many friends, relations and colleagues can you talk casually with about lifelong development and spirituality? With how many of them would it be more appropriate and diplomatic to stay silent? Staying silent about what is important to you is not healthy. It is a form of repression and denial that can affect psychological and physical well-being.

Because the new spirituality is so young, we are still developing its language and its terms. So one reason why some of us may be reluctant to talk about spirituality is not so much that we are diffident or shy, but that, lacking clear terms and concepts, we know we will not be able to communicate clearly, especially if faced with skepticism.

Introduction

"So you're into what you call spirituality. What exactly do you mean?"

This, for me, is also one of the major purposes of this book, to be part of creating a common, useful, and acceptable modern language for spirituality, so that its concepts and principles are a normal part of everyday conversation anywhere and anytime, but especially in education, healthcare, the caring professions, human resources, and management. The three core components of this book—connection, reflection, and service—provide an acceptable framework for conversation in most environments (see "Three Golden Keys" above).

In general, for example, it is not provocative to suggest that spirituality is about connecting with the wonder and energy of nature, cosmos, and existence. This is a good starting point for any spiritual conversation, isn't it? How do you connect with the wonder and energy of life? It affects our health, moods, and well-being. It is an issue that is personally and collectively important. It is a useful inquiry to direct at education, healthcare, government, and business: are we helping people connect with the wonder and energy of life, or blocking it?

Another acceptable topic for general conversation is the whole issue of human growth and development, our lifelong learning. This is surely not just about material goods and material status, but is also to do with developing compassion, wisdom, and consciousness. This conversation, too, is good, positive, and healthy.

Then there is the third spiritual conversation, which is about values and service. It is absolutely acceptable to talk about spirituality as something that guides our values and the major decisions we make in life, that lead us into living a life of value and of service.

"GOD" AND THE WISDOM OF UNKNOWING

A word of caution: I keep repeating this phrase "connect with the wonder and energy." I am using it because in my experience it is a generally acceptable phrase that seems to work well in many different situations, from raucous pagans through to contemplative mystics, and even with atheistic humanists. It does not seem to be provocative.

What I am discussing here is the verbal tap dance we have to do around the whole subject and concept of God—or whatever other word you might prefer, such as mystery, spirit, God, Goddess, Source, Tao, the field, cosmic consciousness, or no word at all. The challenge in all conversations about spirituality is to find the appropriate language, because people usually need reassuring that you are not making assumptions about their beliefs.

For some people the word *God* is just fine, but for many others it is provocative and describes a superstitious and naive idea about a man in the sky who creates and decides everything. There is no "God" in Buddhism, and as one teenager posted on a website bulletin board, "If God is energy why should I accept God as a kind of human? Everything is energy. And because God is energy, God cannot be like Morgan Freeman in a Hollywood movie!"

This teenager—referring to Freeman's role as God in the movies *Bruce Almighty* and *Evan Almighty*—is rightly accusing people of attributing human characteristics to what, in fact, is the whole mystery of creation. And any intelligent child would pose some questions to someone who asserts as a literal fact that "God" created everything (the great Russian doll of theological enquiry): What was there before God? What created God?

There are also traditions, of course, such as paganism, that may believe in many gods.

The new spirituality, however, is comfortable with the deeper mystical idea that the ultimate creation and purpose of life is a mystery and that it is most wise to be comfortable with unknowing. (A good example of this approach can be found in William Johnston's *Mysticism of "The Cloud of Unknowing."*[12] For something more modern, see Karen Armstrong's *The Case for God: What Religion Really Means.*[13]) But, although it is a mystery, it is not a frigid or neutral or negative mystery. Of all things, spirituality asserts that creation is awesome and wonderful.

MYSTERIOUS BUT POSITIVE AND BENEVOLENT

The new spirituality then goes a step further, claiming that existence is not only awesome and wonderful, but is also positive, loving, and benevolent. Notwithstanding the terrible suffering, pain, and fear endured by some, and notwithstanding nature's occasional harshness, there is something essentially good about the whole process of existence.

This claim, that the universe is essentially good and evolving in a positive and beneficent way, is central to spirituality. This benevolence is not put forward as a belief or intellectual proposition, but as a fundamental knowing that sits at the heart of spiritual experience.

Some philosophers may want to argue that the cosmos is balanced between good and evil, or that it is neither good nor bad but neutral. Others will suggest that it is infantile even to apply human judgments, such as good or bad, to creation. But the world's spiritual practitioners—people who choose to spend their lives experiencing and exploring spirituality—assert with great clarity that the cosmos is essentially benevolent. It is permeated with love, not hate.

The Shekinah (glory of the divine presence) in Judaism is beneficent and filled with grace. Buddha consciousness is blissful, not hellish. The Tao (the absolute principle as seen by Chinese philosophy) is an ocean of positive and kind growth, not negative and painful decay. The God of Christianity is one of unconditional love. The mystics of Islam, the Sufis, enjoy the love of God in the way they savor sweet wine and the aroma of desert roses. The ninety-nine names of Allah include the Generous, the Benevolent, and the Compassionate. The Nirvana of Hinduism is bliss.

Meditators and hermits retreat into isolation and decades of self-disciplined practice precisely because the experience is wonderful.

Consciousness expands into compassion and wisdom. The dimension that people discover in spirituality is benevolent and loving. When you yourself connect with the wonder and energy of life, pausing to appreciate the natural world and cosmos, your experience is beneficial, is it not?

Over the decades I have regularly asked students and colleagues this question: When you are in those circumstances where you feel connected to the hum and magic of life, what does it feel like for you? What's going on for you? And they reply with words such as acceptance, beauty, coherence, compassion, connection, forgiveness, goodwill, healing, inspiration, kindness, love, mercy, oneness, and so on. Good, positive things.

In Eastern spiritualities such as Taoism and Tantra, there is clear teaching that we experience all those good things because we are connecting with a vast ocean of benevolent consciousness and energy. In Western faiths, there is a similar idea that we are connecting with God's numinous presence and being, or God's body. This is sometimes, for example, what people mean when they refer to the Holy Ghost or Holy Spirit. Modern mystics sometimes borrow a term from physics and call it the quantum field. (For useful introductions to this subject, see Lynn McTaggarts *The Field*, Ervin Laszlo's *Science and the Akashic Field*, David Bohm's *Wholeness and the Implicate Order*, Fritjof Capra's *Web of Life*, and Adrian B. Smith's *God, Energy and the Field*.[14])

The new spirituality is suffused with this primal *joie de vivre*, based in a universal spiritual experience, that all of us, just because we are alive, are part of a cosmos and a quantum field that is permeated with beneficence; and that, no matter how much we may be hurt or suffering, this is an underlying dimension of our existence and our context.

Part One

CONNECTION

CHAPTER 1

YOUR CONNECTION WITH THE WONDER AND ENERGY OF LIFE

✳

Out of everything in this book and of all the strategies and concepts of the new spirituality, these are perhaps the five most important words: What works best for you?

What kinds of situation and circumstances most easily melt your boundaries, make you more permeable, touch your heart, open your awareness, and connect you with the hum, the wonder and energy of life? Particular environments and circumstances affect you, touch and open you, awaken your spiritual knowing and intuition—and you need to recognize and know what these circumstances are that work for you.

One possible example is the way you might respond to landscape, nature, or water. The ambience of these situations may take you into a different mood—moderately different, but an altered state of consciousness nonetheless. In a quiet and discreet way there is a subtle shift in your awareness and the quality of your experience as you connect with the hum of existence. It feels good. You regain some sanity, some harmony, some focus, some trust. Some of your concerns melt away or are placed in perspective. You have softly and instinctively switched channels and moved into connection.

33

Chapter 1

This is normal spiritual experience. A sense of connection. A change in ambience. A healthy and natural shift in your consciousness and mood. Perhaps very subtle. Perhaps just a whisper.

This minor shift may just seem to be something ordinary to you, like a brief period of relaxation or a lifting of your mood, but ponder more carefully what happens within in those circumstances. Why is there this shift? What has actually happened within you? Surely your heart has been touched and your consciousness expanded, a slight nuance of greater compassion and awareness. More soulful.

Occasionally, people protest to me that they never have experiences like this, but then I ask them if they have experienced special moments of knowing that there is something essentially good and wonderful about life, perhaps, for example, when they have been in a friendly crowd when their football team has won, or lovemaking with their beloved, or lost in a hobby, or with a team of colleagues in full and creative flow, or with a glass of wine and a wonderful book. Finally, they hear something that does indeed work for them—and they smile with recognition.

WHEN DOES IT HAPPEN FOR YOU?

Creation, existence, the cosmos, the natural world—all this is stunning and awesome. It is sensational. I use the word *sensational* here in its true meaning—there are *sensations* and feelings when you experience your connection with all that is. No wonder, for you are part of it. Every cell in your body is alive with it.

But the volume and amplitude of this sense of connection varies. Sometimes the experience may not be there at all for you. At other times it is subtle. And sometimes this sensational experience is obvious, even rapturous and ecstatic.

The difficulty, of course, is that we are human and forget that we live in this extraordinary cosmos; or we ignore it or are too numb to feel it. We are so caught up in the stimulation of our daily lives, so engaged in our immediate circumstances of family, relationships, career, health, and media that we stop noticing the magic of existence. We may also be deadened by the noise and pollution of our urban environments, the endless information, and the drudge of work. There may too be so much *stuff* in our lives that we simply cannot see beyond it. And of course we may also suffer bad moods that may last far too long, even denying that life and creation are in any way good.

All this is not an intellectual issue such as "Do you believe in God?" It is simply about remembering and coming home to your awareness that there is a wonder to life. But people have this awareness in different ways and in different circumstances, and it is important that we understand what the pioneering psychologist and student of religious experience William James a hundred years ago called the "varieties of religious experience."[1]

The most crucial thing I have learned in all my classes and research is that *everyone* without exception has these experiences, but you may not recognize you are having them. There has surely been a moment, or moments, when you have been caught by the beauty or wonder or magic of life. This moment may have been a quiet time alone in landscape or watching your children or being caught by the poignancy and emotion of music. There are a thousand different times when you may have sensed and intuited and felt and thought that there is something more to life than just surface appearances.

When has your heart moved? When have you felt an inner knowing, a haunting or even a wild ecstatic inspiration that there is a marvel and vitality to all life and creation?

These are important experiences. These are the times when, even if you do not know it, you are in a state of connection with the underlying mystery and brilliance of creation, when the usual boundaries of your sense of self become more relaxed and permeable and you feel your relationship with all that is.

Most of the formal research from institutions such as the Alister Hardy Religious Experience Research Centre, the UK's major academic research body studying spiritual experiences, suggests that nature is the major environment in which people have a sense of spiritual connection. But I have found that if the question is asked in a very open way—especially if we start with the proposition that spiritual connection is natural—then the list is far longer and more varied. I have asked this question in hundreds of classes and conversations and these are the kinds of response I have heard:

- I thought that kind of connection only happens to saints in caves. But it happens for me when I'm playing football with my son. And when I'm cooking. I kind of knew something was happening when I went walking by the sea or in the hills. I felt something special. I couldn't put it in words.

- I just need to get away from everyone and everything. I need a completely quiet space. I just sit and wait. I pray that the children leave me alone! And then slowly I begin to feel like myself again and something shifts and I feel all right and that the world is good. I like gardening, too.

- Mad dance! I have to dance. I love raving. It takes me into a state of being completely ecstatic and connected with spirit.

- Reading is very important to me. I also like puzzles. Sitting there, pencil in my mouth, I go into a sort of reverie. The world feels good.

- It doesn't matter what I'm doing. It comes over me unexpectedly. Suddenly I'm just aware of everything, and my breathing is very calm. Is this what they call mindfulness?

- With my animals. I love them.

- I am most deeply in my experience of connection when I'm caring for someone who is in pain. When I witness suffering something moves in my heart, and, it's strange, I can feel the beauty of life too.

Now we'll look at the first of several exercises that will appear regularly throughout the book. You have several choices as you encounter them. You may just read them as part of the ongoing flow of the text. You may choose also to pause for a couple of minutes and give them full attention. Or you may prefer just to read them and come back to them later at your leisure.

EXERCISE
WHEN DOES IT HAPPEN FOR YOU?

Pause for a few moments and look back over your life.

There have been times and circumstances when you have felt a sense of life's magic.

This experience may have been very obvious or very subtle.

It may have lasted a while or touched you for only a few seconds.

Notice and be aware of when this has happened for you.

GATEWAYS TO CONNECTION

What follows now is a list I have put together of the different "Gateways" and circumstances in which many people most easily experience their spiritual connection. They appear in no particular order, except alphabetical. You may not relate to them all.

Look through the entries and see which of them resonates with your own experience. Do not be concerned about whether or not your sense of connection with the magic of life is loud and obvious. Your heart and consciousness may be touched only lightly. The experience may be very subtle.

As you remember which circumstances work for you, pause and remember your feelings and thoughts at the time.

Some Gateways

angels	animals	architecture
aroma	art	being with a beloved
birth	building	caring
celebrating	ceremony	chant
contemplation	cooking	crafts
crisis and suffering	dance	death
divination	drumming	entertaining
flow at work	food	gardening
geometry and math	healing	helping
hobbies	humor	landscape
lovemaking	martial arts	meditation
movement	music	parenting
passage of the seasons	pilgrimage	poetry
prayer	project successfully completed	psychic experiences
reading	risk	sacred space
sharing	song	sound
sport	study	suffering
teaching	theater	touch
walking	work	writing

WHAT IS YOUR SPIRITUAL STYLE?

You can see here that we are liberating spiritual experience and spirituality from the idea that it happens only in religious or sacred circumstances. It may indeed be the case that prayer or religious singing touches your heart and opens you to the wonder of creation, but it may equally be the case that just sitting there watching television is also a circumstance that works as a helpful gateway for you. Certainly in my life I experience moments of connection and heartfelt awareness when I am watching television with my family.

I am not here promoting television as a spiritual practice, but I am saying that it is useful to liberate ourselves from fixed ideas about what is and what is not spiritual. It is not the thing in itself that matters—prayer or television, temple or shopping mall—it is what happens in our hearts and awareness that is important.

But not only are there many different circumstances in which we may experience spirituality, there are also different styles, and we need to be aware of them because these differences can sometimes create confusion and conflict.

You may be moved by music or dance, but what is the style of music you enjoy and in what way do you engage with it? Singing Gregorian chants has a very different contemplative style from emotional gospel singing or tribal chanting. A Tibetan Buddhist monk might be very comfortable with the atmosphere of Christian monastic chant, and vice versa, but neither of these contemplative styles might be comfortable with the noise of a more exuberant form of worship, whether it be Christian, Jewish, or Hare Krishna.

I have not developed a classification of different spiritual styles, but it is obvious that there *are* different styles and it is good to be aware of them, because otherwise they may stimulate cultural prejudices and personality clashes. Meditators may be wary of the noisy and joyful. If you prefer a physical style, such as dance or martial arts, you may dislike the more studious approaches, just as people who connect through service and healing may distrust those who prefer isolation.

It is also good for us to stretch our repertoire and taste different styles. It might be useful for a dignified meditator to try out wild dancing, just as it might be good for a wild dancer to experiment with being still.

SPIRITUAL STYLES

In the list below are some of the different styles and temperaments in which you may practice your spirituality and spiritual connection. It is useful to review them and notice the ones that match your character and temperament.

It is also useful to notice the styles that you feel you might like to explore. Notice too the ones you may have a prejudice against and therefore need perhaps to develop some knowledge and tolerance.

adventurous	ascetic	careful
chaotic	communal	conservative
devotional	disciplined	earnest
ecstatic	emotional	experimental
extrovert	flamboyant	focused
group	innocent	intellectual
introvert	intuitive	joyous
meditative	methodical	philosophical
poetic	practical	psychic
purist	radical	reclusive
relaxed	scattered	scientific
sensuous	studious	touchy

THE ONGOING BACKGROUND HUM

Traditionally, religions tend to suggest that spiritual experience is rare and only for a special few, but here we are reversing that approach. The new spirituality, along with many mystical and shamanic traditions, reframes the idea and suggests that we are perpetually inside a spiritual experience, and all that ever changes is whether or not we are conscious of it. We are like fish in water. But are we aware that we are in it? We hardly notice, for example, the air we breathe or the force of gravity that holds us to the earth, yet they are constantly there. We are also, just because we exist, part of the wonder.

In every new group I teach, I ask whether there are people there who, from childhood, have always been conscious of the fact that there is something special and magical about life—and never lost that knowing. Always several people nod and raise their hands.

There are also other people in these groups who have a moment of revelation as they realize they too have always sensed the spiritual dimension of life, but had never consciously acknowledged it. They just took their experience for granted and did not think it was anything special. They certainly did not label it as "spiritual," but they always had a certain trust in the beauty and magic of creation. They could always feel, despite the challenges and troubles of daily life, this sense of a wider context. There is a simplicity and purity to their experience. Their spiritual experience is also calm, like a subtle but consistent background hum.

You may also be one of those people who have never lost their sense of connection and have felt it, like a soft and ongoing hum in the background, for the whole of your life. I have one friend, Karen, who has always been interested in personal development and spirituality, but, for years, every time she heard people getting excited about their spiritual breakthroughs she did not understand their excitement. This was because from childhood she had always known and felt there was something magical and benevolent about life. For her, it was the most obvious thing in the world. She just could not imagine that other people did not have that same sense. She had maintained her sense of connection despite life's usual challenges—an errant husband, single parenting two boys, financial anxiety.

"But what happens," I asked, "when you've had a row or the boys are playing up or you're exhausted? Surely you forget about the benevolent hum of life then?"

"Of course I do," she agreed, "but, as soon as things are settled, it all comes back to me. I mean, how can I avoid it? It's everything really, isn't it?"

THE NATURE AND DEPTH OF THE EXPERIENCE

If we use food and nourishment as a metaphor, there is often a false expectation that the meal—spirituality—needs always to be some kind of banquet or high cuisine. But meals and food come in many forms: a cup of tea, a raw carrot, beans on toast, nibbling throughout the day, chocolates, and ice cream. And then there are sit-down cooked meals and visits to restaurants and Sunday lunches. Not to mention the cuisines of different regions, from Yorkshire bangers and mash to Tokyo sushi.

It is obvious that food comes in different forms. So too do spirituality and spiritual experience. Our spiritual connections, as I described above, may come in any number of different circumstances and styles, colored and formed by culture and temperament.

But, as well as these different circumstances and styles, spiritual experiences also vary in their duration, volume, and quality. The most highly profiled spiritual experiences are dramatic and peak moments such as Paul meeting God on the road to Damascus or Buddha achieving full enlightenment under the Bodhi tree. The academic literature on religious experience is nearly always focused on these intense and life-changing encounters with the numinous.

But there are also many people who do not have these intense moments of numinous awakening but, as I described above, live with an ongoing background hum of the magic, their hearts almost permanently in a gentle space of compassion. Brian Thorne, a leading professor of spiritual counseling, describes, for example, how, since he was a child, he always knew that he was loved and in a universe that was benevolent.[2]

Others of us, however, may be touched intermittently and only subtly with just a fleeting moment of recognition, a subtle intimation.

In a bad mood, for instance, you may glimpse something that momentarily touches your heart and connects you with the magic of life. For just a brushing second you are reminded of life's beauty. You may too, for example, be in the middle of a busy office job and someone cracks a wry joke or says something insightful; or you see a cloud against blue sky through the window; or you hear a bar of music. In the midst of that hectic day, a gap opens up in the momentum and a knowing that there is a wonder to life flickers within you. Your soul lights up. And then you get on with your work.

You can see then that there are several different aspects to anyone's experience of spiritual connection and that each of these aspects will vary greatly. For the sake of clarity, we can summarize them:

Your gateways: the kind of circumstances and triggers, such as landscape, dance, prayer, and so on.

Your style: the type of character and mood, such as fiery, contemplative, devotional, and so on.

The volume: the power and intensity of the experience, ranging from an ecstatic meltdown to a soft brush of knowing.

The duration: how long the experience lasts, from a second to the background hum of a lifetime.

The meaningfulness: the extent to which the experience impacts upon you and deepens your general sense of spirituality, which we will explore more fully later.

I have a real love and passion for this way of looking at spiritual connection, because it liberates us from any kind of monopoly or enthrallment. This is a very fluid and open approach. It is not attached to any particular method or expectancy, so how you practice your spirituality does not have to fit into anyone else's boxes. You do not have to meet the expectations of any organized spiritual group or religion. Most of all you do not have to satisfy any of your own preconceived notions or expectations about what your spiritual experience should be like.

EXERCISE

RECALLING A MOMENT OF CONNECTION

Take a few moments of quiet.

Perhaps you can remember a moment when you were touched by the wonder and beauty of life. When was it?

Remember the circumstances.

Remember too how it felt—your emotions, your thoughts.

How long did it last?

How powerful was it?

Did it have any impact on your life?

THE ELITISM THAT MAKES CONNECTION SEEM DIFFICULT

I wrote in the section above that religions often portray spiritual experiences as being special events that happen only to special people. This distinction is part of a more general cultural understanding that spiritual experiences are either rare or intense. It is important to name and deconstruct these old and disempowering concepts, because they lurk like ghosts in our spiritual culture, sometimes frightening people away from their own natural and inherent spirituality.

Hierarchy

First, there is the problem of the hierarchies and organizations usually associated with the world's major religions, whose organizational structures are similar to and sometimes copied from the military, with the masses at the bottom, officers above them, and, at the apex, a supreme general or emperor. You can see this in churches and temples, with the people organized in rows, then priests, and then at the top, just below God or Cosmic Consciousness, you will find a supreme bishop, rabbi, rimpoche, shaman, and so on. In some cultures there was, of course, an actual merging of religious, political, and military structures, so that the monarch or emperor was head of all three. The current monarch of the United Kingdom is still known as "Defender of the Faith." For the last two hundred years the office of Dalai Lama has been both a religious and a political role.

This hierarchy is then reflected in doctrines, which suggest that the priests have some kind of exclusive relationship with God or the gods or Cosmic Consciousness, that only a few special and ordained people can have access to spiritual experience, and the rest of us, tainted by original sin or ignorance or karma, are unfit for such a direct experience.

The new spirituality asserts clearly that, just because you are alive, you are an intrinsic and inescapable part of creation's wonder. And nobody has any privileges.

Discipline and Unworthiness

This elitism is also often accompanied by the doctrine that spiritual connection itself is really difficult to attain and requires a lengthy process of discipline, self-sacrifice, and purification. The suggestion here is that a high personal price has to be paid before you can experience your spiritual connection. You need to be a spiritual athlete.

There are many ways of paying this price. In shamanic traditions, for example, people need time alone in the wilderness. Many forms of Buddhism require extended meditation. Some Christian traditions require retreat, intense prayer, and abstention from all bodily pleasures, including food and sex.

All of this spiritual athleticism is accompanied by the well-known suggestions that we are inherently unworthy. In Islam, Judaism, and Christianity, we can find teachings stating that we are all tainted by original sin and have fallen from grace. In Eastern faiths, our unworthiness is clothed in the idea that we are all tainted by karma and our past lives as animals. In Hinduism, for example, this idea feeds into a caste system, untouchables at the bottom and an elite Brahman caste at the top.

These types of idea tend to belittle everyone's natural spiritual connection. They ignore the simple reality that life throbs within all of us and that spirit is in everything. The new spirituality is clear that it is normal to be aware of our cosmic context. We are in it, just as a fish is in water or a bird is in the air.

Peak Experiences

Then there is all the academic research around spiritual experiences, which also feeds into this elitism by nearly always describing and categorizing spiritual experiences as if they were unusual and rare.

Starting with William James's classic *The Varieties of Religious Experience*, followed by nearly all books on the subject, the research data tends usually to be focused on dramatic events.[3] One moment the individual is in a normal psychological and social state, and the next moment—due, for example, to drugs or surgery or exquisite landscape or just a spontaneous occurrence—that person is startled out of normal daily consciousness into an altered state so that he or she now perceives the world in a completely new way and in a completely changed mood.

It is true that some people do indeed have these types of startling spiritual experience, but it is misleading to suggest that these are the usual and only way people experience their spirituality. Worse than misleading, however, this focus on extraordinary experiences and awakenings suggests that these dramatic moments are the only valid way you may connect with spirit. Because of this, you may invalidate and even ignore the actual less noisy spiritual experiences you do have. Or, to put it another way, you may think that spiritual experiences *must* be unusual and extraordinary, and anything less is not spiritual.

This approach ignores the reality that the hum and magic of life are always there, in and around us. In this and the following chapter, I illustrate how, in fact, most of us have a varying range of spiritual experiences, as we dip in and out according to our mood and circumstances.

Style, Tone, and Language

Finally, there are the style, tone, and language often associated with faith and belief. People often speak about spirituality in a tone of voice and with a body language they do not use in ordinary, daily life. Often I have observed people talking about religion in a precious and earnest style, as if whispering about the world's greatest secret in a very strict library.

This style of conversation also implies that spiritual connection is rare and special and not to be sullied by a normal tone of voice and normal behavior. All across the world, priests talk about spirituality in their temples and churches in what can only be described as a "priestly" manner, often satirized by comics, provided they are not frightened off by the possible consequences of blasphemy.

At the same time there is also a built-in elitism to the language of spirituality, of which I myself am guilty. I am not sure if there is a solution. It rests in the kind of words we use to describe spiritual

47

experience and connection. These are all superlative words with implicit exclamation marks. Wonder. Mystery. Awe. Existence. Creation. Bliss. Ecstasy. Exclamation mark. Exclamation mark. These words are beautiful and accurate in their own way, but they also shore up this business of spiritual experience being special and extraordinary, and therefore in some way not easily accessible to all of us.

We may find the same elitism in the art or food world. Some gourmets, for example, might be snobbish about haute cuisine and appear not to recognize the value of bangers and mash or fish and chips. But it is obviously ignorant to suggest that only a Michelin three-star meal is valid food.

It is not helpful to suggest that the only spirituality worth experiencing are peak experiences with bells, whistles, and flashing lights, rare and exceptional, restricted to special and exceptional people. That is not the case. There are many ways we achieve spiritual nourishment, and perhaps the most deserving of attention are those quiet people who maintain a constant hum of connection and benevolent awareness, not those who are particularly eloquent and occasionally inspired.

THE ORTHODOX JEW AND THE DEVOUT MUSLIM

Focusing on the normality, circumstances, and styles of spiritual experience is liberating and creative. It releases us into a world of shared experience. Let me illustrate this with a story from one of my students, Andrew, a successful businessman who regularly attended meetings of his local chamber of commerce. The downsides to these meetings were his frequent encounters with an Orthodox Jew and a devout Muslim, with whom the conversations were always difficult. He never knew what to say to them, and his nightmare was that he might have to sit next to one of them through a whole meal. But, after attending one of my courses, he wondered what would happen if he asked the two men what best connected them with the wonder and energy of life, with God.

A few weeks later he had an opportunity when he met them at another chamber-of-commerce event. It was the usual scene, people standing around, chatting and drinking their tea and coffee. He spoke with the Orthodox Jew about local politics and business for a while and then said, "Might I ask you a question about your religion? Would that be OK?"

The Orthodox Jew frowned and then agreed.

"I was wondering," Andrew asked, "when do you feel closest to the wonder and energy of life? What part of your life or your religion best connects you with the spirit of existence, with God?"

"With the wonder and energy? With God?" he asked. The man now smiled. Being a good family man was important to him, he replied. Caring for his wife and children and his parents touched his heart and connected him. He liked the family rituals, too, such as the Sabbath blessing of the evening meal. There were also scriptures that inspired him, and he enjoyed being alone in the synagogue, sitting quietly in contemplation.

The two men connected in this conversation and created a positive rapport.

Then, a little while later, Andrew found himself with the devout Muslim, and he began exactly the same conversation.

"I was wondering when you feel the closest to the wonder and energy of life. What part of your life or your work most easily connects you with God? What is it in Islam that particularly touches your heart and opens you up?"

The Muslim smiled too. "When do I feel the blessing of Allah? Why do you ask?"

"I'm interested in people's paths. All their paths," Andrew responded. "I myself connect when I am out in nature and also when I do my martial-arts practice. It's good for me. Good for my body and my soul. What works best for you in your faith? What is good for you?"

The Muslim replied that he was always particularly touched by the rhythm and poetic cadence of the Koran, when he read it to himself and also when he heard others reciting it. He also felt connected to God when he was doing charitable work in the community organized by his mosque.

Again the two men relaxed into an enjoyable conversation, building friendship and rapport.

EXERCISE
A BRIDGE-BUILDING CONVERSATION

Is there someone you know who has spiritual beliefs very different from yours?

Imagine yourself having a conversation with this person.

Imagine that the ambience is friendly.

In a way that is respectful and appropriate, you ask this person what it is in their faith or spirituality that most touches their heart and connects them with the source of their inspiration.

Imagine yourself starting this inquiry and conversation in a way that is completely acceptable to this person.

Contemplate how interesting and inspiring this conversation can be and how it builds bridges between you.

Be open to the wide diversity of experience in which all people experience their spiritual connection.

THE DEPTH OF YOUR SPIRITUALITY

"With all this diversity and pick-'n'-mix spiritual choice, people who are engaged in the new spirituality never go deep. You are like consumers in a supermarket filling your basket with what you fancy. What you need is to develop depth within one particular tradition."

I have heard this comment many times from people from many different spiritual traditions. They themselves are usually rooted in a single approach, and this rootedness works well for them. But it is unfair and inaccurate to claim that we all need to spend time deep in a specific spiritual path.

What we do need, however, is to spend more time and give more awareness to deepening our sense of connection with the magic and love and creative energy of life. This does not happen just inside formal spiritual situations, such as in a temple or during meditation, but happens all the time in many different ways. We can open our hearts and expand our benevolent awareness in all circumstances.

Again, we need to take seriously the answers to the question "What works best for you?" There is no sense in following the same spiritual path as our parents if it does not develop our compassion and our connection. Equally, we may well be inspired by the personas of spiritual leaders and teachers, but there is little point in adopting their spiritual practices if they do not work for us.

We want to create a spirituality that integrates and is part of our everyday life at work, at home, socially, and in our communities. The only way to do this is through a very personal and private self-management in which we take responsibility for how we guide our spiritual lives.

And life itself is a kaleidoscope of diversity.

In this moment, there is the miracle of the heat and the movement in our bodies. There is the magic of the written word. Around us are meaningful objects and people and animals. Beneath us and around us is the wonder of a beautiful planet, spinning and orbiting. Maybe you are touched, too, by the genius and poignant tragedy of human society. Perhaps you can hear birdsong or see the sky. All of these— and more—are a natural part of your spirituality.

So—spiritual depth is a very individual and interior dimension that you, and you alone, assess according to your own lights and not according to the worldview of others. Nevertheless, there are certain core strategies you can use to manage and guide your spiritual experience, regardless of your circumstances or style, which we now need to explore.

CHAPTER 2

DEEPENING YOUR EXPERIENCE

✴

Throughout history and in all cultures, people have wanted to guide, manage, and deepen their moments of spiritual connection and awakening so that they do not occur just serendipitously or haphazardly. It is beautiful, touching, and inspiring when we experience these times that open our hearts and expand our consciousness, but how much better it might be if we could deliberately create and guide these experiences.

Spiritual cultures across the world have therefore developed circumstances and techniques so that seekers can trigger spiritual connection in a planned and coherent way, and also guide the experience so that it lasts longer and is more powerful. Spiritual travelers can then linger in the experience, become accustomed to it, understand it better, and allow their hearts and consciousness to contemplate and explore its meaning and dimensions.

A well-known and widely used strategy, for example, is music. From Christian hymns and classical music, through gongs and tribal drums to rock concerts, it is well understood that music and rhythm, especially if experienced over a long period of time and in a heartfelt way, will take most people into an altered state of consciousness and a sense of spiritual connection. Hearts open. Minds calm down. People feel part of the community of life.

Another well-known example is the understanding that the natural world enables spiritual experience even in the most cynical. The harshest of professed atheists will melt at the wonder of a glorious sunset.

And another example, found all over the world, is that of being in silence.

But all three of these spiritual strategies—music, nature, and silence—have something in common. The more often and the longer you do them, the deeper your spiritual experience becomes, the more your heart opens and your consciousness wakes up. Five minutes with a sunset is good, but a month in the mountains or by the ocean of course goes deeper. Five minutes of calm silence can help, but twenty minutes of quiet also has a more profound effect, especially if experienced daily.

These examples demonstrate two techniques or skills that are universally used for cooperating with, guiding, and amplifying spiritual experience—repetition and duration. Whatever it is that works for you—nature, art, sport, music, reading, prayer, and so on—the more time you spend doing it, the more your experience will deepen and improve, and the better you will get at it.

In the last chapter we explored the different gateways and styles that might work best for you. So here is a straightforward and graceful key to developing your own spirituality: *assess what works best to open your heart and connect you, and then do it regularly and often.*

Because experiencing spiritual connection is enjoyable, essentially you are being asked to repeat things that you enjoy. Doesn't this cheer you up? This approach gives you permission and actually encourages you to do what you enjoy in order to develop your spirituality—a rare idea for people brought up to think of religion as being stern and curtailing pleasure.

The new spirituality encourages like a friendly coach: connect with spirit in the way that is easiest for you. Get on with it. Do it. You know it is good for you.

Exercise:
WHAT CIRCUMSTANCES MOST ATTRACT YOU?

Again, contemplate the situations and circumstances in which you most easily experience a spiritual connection.

Which of them would be easiest for you to repeat regularly and often?

Which of them attracts you most?

Begin to formulate a plan for actually putting yourself again into those situations and circumstances that support your spirituality.

When and where would it be easiest for you to do them?

INTRODUCING THE FOUR CORE SKILLS

So, let us assume now that you have an idea about what types of circumstances enable you most easily to feel your spiritual connection, whether it is watching television with the family, playing golf, walking out in nature—whatever works best for you.

There are now four important and crucial practical skills you need for deepening and amplifying your spiritual connection. They are simple, easy to practice, and can be used by everyone. In one form or another you will find them in most spiritual traditions, and this, again, is one of the great merits of the new spirituality, that with a global overview we can discern these universal strategies. I remember how inspiring and reassuring it was for me when I found these techniques surfacing in almost every tradition I explored. I was surprised because I had not expected there to be core similarities in the practices, for example, of Christian contemplative prayer and tribal dancing, or Jewish Kabbala and Amazonian shamans, but these same skills are always there in wise and effective spiritual practice.

These four core skills are relevant and supportive regardless of your style and circumstances. They are the skills of being able to:

- pause and be mindful;

- relax, center, and ground in your body;

- observe what is happening in a kind and good-humored way; and

- yield to the feeling of connection.

Before I describe them in greater detail, let me immediately share two stories that will help to explain them.

THE PRIESTS WHO WERE NOT CONNECTED

Usually I work with groups made up of people from a variety of religious backgrounds and beliefs, but occasionally I find myself with men and women from a single-faith community. This first story is about an encounter that took place during a one-day course on spiritual practice I led for fifty Anglican clergy.

Being with these men and women was enjoyable because they were all openhearted, intelligent, and dedicated to their caring and pastoral work.

Of course, part of their job description, like that of all priests in all faiths, is to connect regularly with the magic of creation and enable others too to have their own connection with it. Yet when we talked about their actual lifestyle and state of connection, we learned they were mainly exhausted, some burning out, overwhelmed by too much work, and, most poignantly of all, disconnected from the wonder and energy of existence.

To begin the day, I led them in a meditation, which took them into the exercise of listing all those circumstances in which they most easily connect with the beauty and mystery of creation, with God. They came up with lists that covered most of the gateways and styles described in the previous chapter. Landscape, music, families, and solitude featured prominently.

What surprised me, though, was that their lists missed some of the core elements of their faith. None of them listed prayer. And no one listed the very heart of Christian worship, the ceremony of the Eucharist or Holy Communion. This act of worship may be unfamiliar to you, but for many Christians it is a supreme moment when they can commune with God and Jesus through the evocative ritual of sharing bread and wine that represent Jesus' body and blood. It is a moment of pure connection. But it was not on the vicars' lists of circumstances that connected them and opened their hearts.

"What about the Eucharist?" I asked. "What happens when you're celebrating Communion? What happens for you when you're down on your knees or bowing, holding the bread and then the wine, offering them to Christ? Are you not connected then?"

The conversation that followed my enquiry was intimate, realistic, and poignant. I was surprised by the commonality of their experience. None of them were experiencing any sense of connection during this most holy of Christian moments. We discussed whether this was because they no longer believed in it or valued it, but these were definitely not the reasons. They were, in fact, distracted and overwhelmed.

"I'm too busy doing my job," one shared. "For example, I might be thinking about the woman who arranged the altar flowers and reminding myself to thank her. She's a tricky customer on my church council, and I need her vote to approve the new nursery in the church hall."

There were nods of understanding and sympathy from the other clergy. The Eucharist had become just another part of their working day, alongside the pastoral work; the local politics; the church politics; the administration; the preparation of sermons, newsletters, and calendars; and community building. Like so many modern people, they were generally overwhelmed by their jobs.

I guided the conversation so that they remembered what had called them into the church in the first place. It was, they remembered, not just the pastoral and community work that had attracted them. At core, their calling had been a very personal experience of Jesus' message, of God, and of the wonder of life. During their training for ordination, they had all been touched and inspired by Holy Communion, and immediately after ordination they had all felt humble and proud that they were now able to lead this precious ceremony.

But the pressures of the job had seeped through to all of them. I have seen the same loss of connection in many different milieux, where men and women begin their careers motivated and energized by the wonder of life, only to lose it to the daily grind and oppressive pressure. But it is particularly poignant and paradoxical when clergy, who are supposed to be the specialists in connection, lose their connection—not through a crisis of faith but through the demands of their lifestyle.

USING THE FOUR CORE SKILLS IN COMMUNION

The conversation with the clergy continued for a while, and they began fully to acknowledge what had happened to them over the years. For many of them this was the first time they had spoken to someone else about their predicament. For many it was also the first time they fully acknowledged how disconnected they had become. There was also some shock as they realized it was a general problem in the church and that they were in a room with many others who shared exactly the same experience.

The discussion slowed down, and the group became thoughtful and silent. I suggested that we stay in silence for a few minutes and allow the conversation to settle. I then led a visualization exercise, which used each of the four core skills: (1) pause and be mindful;

(2) relax, center, and ground in body; (3) observe what is happening in a kind and good-natured way; (4) yield to the feeling of the experience.

First, I asked them to visualize, think about, and contemplate the Eucharist. I suggested that they imagine themselves in their churches, kneeling before their altars and holding first the bread and then the wine of Communion. Speaking slowly, I said:

Imagine and sense yourself kneeling or bowing before the altar.

You pause in that moment and still yourself.

You bring your attention fully and mindfully to where you are and what you are doing. *Pause and be mindful.*

You slow down and calm your breathing. You allow yourself to relax. You allow your stomach and chest to relax and sink. You take a slow, quiet breath down into your lower abdomen. Generally, you relax and calm your breath. *Relax, center, and ground your body.*

You now guide your attitude so that it becomes detached, witnessing, observant, and compassionate; benevolent, philosophical, and good-natured. *Observe what is happening in a kind and good-natured way.*

You are aware of the magic of the moment, as you hold the chalice and the bread. There has been a shift in the atmosphere. You have a subtle sense of God's presence, of the wonder and energy.

Allow the experience to enter you more fully. Yield and surrender to it. *Yield to the feeling of the experience.*

The atmosphere in our training room tangibly transformed into a deeper and more meaningful silence as everyone, through the exercise, moved into spiritual connection. We stayed immersed in the silence for several minutes, and then slowly we came out of the exercise. Everyone was moved by the experience.

In the conversation afterward, an ex–rugby player and army chaplain said simply, "I know what I'll do now. I'll spend an extra few seconds pausing in the middle of the Eucharist. I'll gift myself a few moments of grateful presence. I'll allow myself to feel it. I'll do it properly."

His sentiments were echoed around the room. They all recognized their own personal need to pause and be more mindful, centered, and sensitive to the actual experience. To absorb it.

NATURE AND INSTINCTIVE GRATITUDE

The rugby-playing vicar had grasped the essence quickly. It is not rocket science. To deepen our spiritual connection, you have to learn these four simple skills—be mindful, embodied, kindly watchful, and yielding to the feeling.

Let me now share this second story in which we can see these skills being used instinctively by someone who, until he and I talked, had no idea that he was using them. His story may also be similar to your own experience, in that you have a natural and instinctive spirituality, but up until now you have not been aware of it, or no one has ever recognized this in you and validated you.

I met this man when I was working with a group of educators, social workers, and community activists who were exploring how best to integrate spirituality into their work. I began the session in the usual way, asking them to make a list of the circumstances in which they most easily connected with the wonder and energy of life. I then found myself paired up and talking with this man, who walked regularly in the Yorkshire Dales—his home backed on to them—and who was daily seduced by the beauty of the landscape and nature.

He was quick to tell me that spirituality was not his thing and that he had only come to this training out of curiosity. In fact, he said, he was usually suspicious of anything religious.

"I don't really have spiritual experiences," he said, "and I have no idea how to deepen them even if I did have them. I know nothing about this business."

"I wonder if that's true," I said. "When you see a particularly beautiful view, do you pause to enjoy it more?"

"Of course I do."

"And do you sometimes take a deeper breath or gasp, and then find you relax more?"

"I do."

"And," I asked, "do you sometimes feel a sense of appreciation or gratitude for what you can see and feel?"

"I do," he replied again.

Instinctively, this man was doing precisely what he needed to do in order to deepen his experience. In exactly the same way as I had led the exercise with the vicars, he was instinctively pausing, becoming mindful and relaxing his body, and then yielding to the feelings of the experience.

EXERCISE
REMEMBER AND APPRECIATE

Contemplate a situation in which you were momentarily caught by the beauty or magic of the situation. (1) *Pause and be mindful.*

You may have instinctively taken a breath or gasped or sighed. (2) *Relax, center, and ground in your body.*

You then paused and, momentarily or longer, you appreciated the circumstances. (3) *Observe what is happening in a kind and good-natured way.*

Spend a while now contemplating how, in that situation, you were naturally and instinctively sensing and cooperating with your spiritual connection. (4) *Yield to the feeling of the experience.*

Chapter 2

TOWARD A BIOLOGY OR SCIENCE OF SPIRITUAL EXPERIENCE

Our connection with the wonder and energy, with the field, with "God's body," is a felt experience as we creatures of nature and the universe, creatures of flesh and blood, of chemistry, electricity, and magnetism, register that we are fully *alive* and that we are inextricably part of this extraordinary universe. When we connect with our cosmic and natural context, we experience feelings, emotions, thoughts, instincts, and insights that transcend our usual concerns and egocentricity.

In the academic arena of sociobiology, which studies how our inherited biology affects our psychological and social behavior, this phenomenon—our response to the natural world, from a blade of grass out to the mystery of an infinite cosmos—is known as *biophilia*, which translates as "love of nature." Edmund Wilson, the most well-known scholar associated with this research, suggests that biophilia is the source of our religious instinct. He suggests that it derives from the fact that we all emerge from the same event, or Big Bang, that created everything that exists in the cosmos. Because everything comes from this same source, we therefore have a primal and innate connection with all things in the natural world, so, when we connect with nature and cosmos, we are reassured and encouraged by this fundamental connection. Hence, of course, the well-known healing power of nature.[1]

One day perhaps there may be a scientific instrument that measures and explains precisely how we connect with our cosmic source and nature, but at the moment there is no such equipment. There is only the consistent evidence of people's actual lived experience in all cultures and epochs.

There are perhaps, though, the beginnings of some understanding of the biological processes in the two scientific domains of psychoneuroimmunology (PNI) and neurotheology (see glossary). PNI is particularly focused on the relationship between the brain, the nervous system, and the endocrine system, exploring the biological basis of thinking, feeling, and moods—what Candace Pert, a leading researcher in the field, called "the molecules of emotion."[2]

One area of PNI that is particularly relevant to spirituality is the focus on those hormones and neurotransmitters responsible for the "spiritual" feelings of relaxation, pleasure, and even bliss, such as serotonin, oxytocin, and—my own field of expertise—endorphins.[3]

Neurotheology, sometimes also called biotheology or spiritual neuroscience, is the area of research looking at the neural and brain activity that accompanies spiritual experience, visions, and altered states of consciousness. At one point, there was some research suggesting that spiritual experience was purely the result of brain activity, which could be stimulated in a laboratory setting, and there was a well-publicized contention, later found to be unsustainable, that researchers had found the "God spot."[4] An appropriate electric prod to the brain tissue, it was claimed, could induce anyone into a direct experience of God. In fact, all that had been discovered was that certain areas of the brain that were activated by various kinds of social intercourse were also activated when believers were asked to think about God.[5]

COOPERATING WITH A REAL EXPERIENCE

There is, however, something unambiguous and very helpful in all this scientific research, because it shows how the four skills of pausing, relaxing and centering, watching, and yielding to the sensations function. This approach demonstrates that spiritual experience is not just something that is imagined or created in the brain, but that it is a more general experience accompanied by distinct biological, neural, and endocrinologic changes. It is not a head-trip, conjured up by overactive neural synapses.

To state it more explicitly: when you have a sense of spiritual connection, when your heart softens, when your tension releases, and when you become more aware of the wonder of all life, all this is a felt and sensational experience. It is a shift in your hormonal and neural state. Therefore, if you want to manage the experience, you must pay attention to your physical body and its biological state.

This information is also crucial because it also begins to explain, in a logical and coherent way, how spirituality supports well-being and health care, triggering those neural and endocrinologic states that are also the foundation for a healthy immune system and sense of well-being. To be precise, spiritual connection relaxes tissue, creates actual sensations of pleasure, and allows a healthier flow of what is needed to support good health such as, for example, oxygenated blood and antibodies.[6]

All of this explains why these four core skills of spirituality—pausing, embodying, watching, and yielding—are actually effective. They enable you to give precise awareness to how your body is actually experiencing your spiritual connection and then to cooperate with the experience and guide it. As the narrator says in *Conversations with God*, "God communicates through feelings." With these four skills, you are directly cooperating with and guiding those feelings.[7]

This type of awareness and cooperation is also completely normal in practices such as spiritual healing, yoga, body prayer, tantra, and tai chi. The logic is attractive. If you want to cooperate with and deepen your experience, you have to develop awareness of the actual sensations of spiritual experience and then guide them.

Let us now look at each of these four skills in more detail so that you can better use them.

CORE SKILL NO. 1: PAUSE AND BE MINDFUL

The first skill that you need is to be able to pause and notice mindfully what is happening. Without this skill, none of the others can be put into operation.

There you are in a moment of spiritual connection. The right circumstances have occurred—whatever they are—and you have a sense of the magic and wonder of existence. The sky is beautiful. Your children are beautiful. Your team has won. You're touched by some music or by someone's kindness or by some poignancy.

Your feeling of connection may be a gentle hum or something stronger.

You could just be casual about the experience and let it pass by, or you can mindfully cooperate with it and be fully present to its gifts.

To cooperate with this experience and deepen it or explore it, you need to press your pause button and notice it properly. You need to stop. Wake up. Be more aware. Be conscious and recognize that something good is happening.

This sounds easy, and it *is* easy, but I know hundreds of students and colleagues who are explicitly into spirituality but consistently forget to pause and really enjoy these moments.

I have a colleague, Jane, for example, an intellectual who loves studying geometry and sacred architecture in places like Stonehenge, the Great Pyramid, and Chartres Cathedral. She has a wonderful library of books and videos on the subject, and she often visits these beautiful and evocative places, filming and recording them. She loves them. She says that sacred geometry is her spiritual path. Whenever I meet her, she talks enthusiastically about her latest insight and inspiration. But she speeds through these places and is always so busy and bustling.

Her spiritual experience could be so much deeper if she just occasionally paused, became mindful, sank down into her body, relaxed a bit, breathed calmly, and allowed herself a full hit of the magic. Her busyness is especially ironic because these sacred places she loves were specifically constructed so as to amplify spiritual connection. All she has to do is just stand still in them and breathe in a softer style.

Then there is my friend who works full time in an interfaith project. He knows that the wonder and magic are always there in the background. He even pauses for a few seconds every now and again, allowing himself a small taste of connection. This is good, but his emotional and physical well-being would be so enhanced if he gave himself a longer pause to deepen the rapport. He says that he does not have the time.

On the other hand, there are many people who have no education in spiritual practice, but who do instinctively pause. They notice when there is something magical going on in their circumstances, and they allow themselves to pause and register the situation.

Prodding us to be conscious and present to our spiritual experience, many teachings carry the same message. *Wake up. Be here now. Be present.* The tenth-century Indian mystic and philosopher Abhinavagupta said to his students, "Listen carefully. Stop holding on to this or that, inhabit your true absolute nature, and *peacefully* enjoy the essence of what it is to be alive."

To pause and be mindful does not mean that you actually have to stop physical movement. The pause is psychological and mental. The pause is in your consciousness. So, if you are enjoying dancing or singing or white-water rafting or cooking or walking, you can stay in the movement. All that happens is that, simultaneously and elegantly multitasking, you become conscious of what you are doing. Enjoying yourself, but enjoying it with awareness, with mindfulness.

Pausing mindfully was the very first strategy needed by the vicars in their worship. Only then could they appreciate the magic of their circumstances.

It Can Be Difficult to Pause

Some people, however, do not want to pause and be mindful because they fear it will sabotage their flow, especially if they experience spiritual connection in circumstances that involve movement, such as dance or sport. But they then learn that pausing does not sabotage the experience, but deepens it.

"When I experience the beauty of landscape," one student shared, "I become excited and inspired. I feel energized and I want to express this through dance or running or poetry. Originally I was put off pausing and being mindful because it demanded, it seemed to me, that I come out of this energized space. But then I learned how to pause mentally and be fully in the moment. It's fantastic. The whole experience sinks deeply into me."

A young man who loved dancing at all-night raves and who then joined a shamanic study group also illustrates this.

"It was wonderful," he said, "getting lost in the trance and the zone, and just moving my body with the pulse of everyone else on the dance floor. I was out of my head. Literally. Ecstatic. Not ready to crash out, still buzzing, I'd still be awake at dawn. . . . But the shamanic training taught me to dance and *at the same time* be awake and aware. It's a whole different dimension. When I'm dancing now, I can feel spirit throbbing inside me. I can really be present with it. It's a different dimension. A completely different way of being alive."

Becoming mindful, however, is difficult when we are running excited or nervous energy. Pausing can feel very uncomfortable, like putting the brakes on when we are driving too fast. They screech. This is because we are stopping the momentum of adrenaline-fuelled emotions and thoughts, which are moving forward at their own pace and velocity. Bringing them to a halt creates temporary sensations of irritability, impatience, and even nausea.

To take a mental pause, to be calmly aware—this is a new dynamic, a new attitude, a new chemistry, a new set of neural grooves. Literally and physically, there is real friction as our nervous and endocrine systems have to slow down and integrate the new mood. This recognition is why, for example, the National Health Service in the UK has been exploring using mindfulness meditation techniques as an adjunct to cognitive behavioral therapy. This ability to pause and watch what is happening provides oases of sanity in what might otherwise be distressing mental conditions.[8]

Here is where repetition is so helpful. If you have the discipline to pause regularly and become mindful, its practice becomes much easier. It is like exercising and building a spiritual muscle. You build a new neuroendocrinologic groove, embedding in your habitual patterns a new and ongoing behavior and attitude.

Many tribal peoples also have a useful wisdom here, especially for young people who enjoy activity and excitement. Before taking their people into times of ceremony and spiritual connection, many indigenous and tribal groups often use dances that last many hours, or even days, to make sure everyone has shaken off and used up their excess nervous energy. Comfortably fatigued, people can then pause and yield more easily to the spiritual dimension.

The Indian guru Osho similarly had his students dancing, shaking, laughing, and even making love until their excess energy was spent and they could then surrender gracefully to being calm and connected to the field. This practice is reflected, too, in many movement and dance classes, where it is in the quiet time at the end of the class that you may finally feel a sense of calm, mindfulness, and spiritual rapport.

EXERCISE
MINDFULNESS

Take a few quiet minutes.

Bring into your awareness a situation in which you know you usually experience a sense of spiritual connection.

Visualize, imagine, sense yourself in the middle of that situation.

Imagine that, while you are in it, you take a mental pause.

You pause and notice with full consciousness that something special is happening to you.

For a few seconds you allow yourself to be aware of the moment and the experience.

CORE SKILL NO. 2: RELAX, CENTER, AND GROUND

Your whole body is the organ of perception, which recognizes, senses, and experiences your spiritual connection, but these sensations and feelings are often subtle.

This subtlety is problematic because there are usually other stimulations in your life that are louder. Some come from outside in the form of noise or, for example, from your children needing breakfast. Some come from inside you in the form of thoughts and emotions, which can also dominate your attention.

All across the world, spiritual culture by spiritual culture, the solution to this noise is always the same. You have to take your awareness and center of gravity out of your head and down into your body. In the classic language of spirituality, you have to be grounded, earthed and embodied. Or, in the language of mysticism, your soul, your spiritual awareness, needs to incarnate and inhabit the whole of your temple, your body.

There is a huge difference between being up in your head and top heavy, and being grounded, embodied, and earthed. It feels very different. To be embodied is a balanced and healthy state. It is that comfortable state you experience after a satisfying meal when you are just sitting comfortably, relaxed and sunk into your body. Content. Satisfied. It also happens after good lovemaking. It happens often too on the tenth day of your holiday when finally you relax and remember what it feels like to be human and normal.

Your center of gravity sinks down from your head and fully into your corporeal being, like those images of happy fat monks in both

Christianity and Buddhism. Being anchored in our bodies also creates a stabilizing center of gravity. This embodiment is called *hara* in martial arts and is the foundation too of much Eastern health care. *Hara* is explicitly taught as the foundation of martial arts and of good horse and motorcycle riding. In old English it used to be called *bottom*, a word still used today to describe a horse rider who has a low sense of gravity and a stable foundation in the saddle.

Good bottom supports us in staying calm and watchful, when otherwise we might be wobbling from overstimulation and anxiety. Later in the book we will also see how it is crucial both for self-development and also for being a kind and reassuring presence to others.

All this is important because, to repeat, this vital understanding, this spiritual experience is visceral, sensational and full of feeling. If you are not grounded in your body, you cannot feel the spiritual experience fully. Half of my work with the vicars, for example, and with most of my students is to keep reminding them to relax and sink into their bodies, so they can sense and be present to what is happening.

As you relax and sink into your body, you can more easily feel the subtle sensations of your spiritual experience, instead of being distracted by endless thoughts and stimulations.

Many spiritual techniques have been developed in many different traditions to help you be embodied and centered. There are many exercises, for instance, that use visualization and imagination to sense a connection between your body and the earth beneath you. And there are many grounding techniques, such as sensing that you have roots extending from the base of your spine and the soles of your feet deep down into the ground.

In martial arts, tai chi (a soft and slow form of martial art), and qi gung (free-flowing healing movement), embodiment is taught through a process of consciously allowing your abdomen to relax and sink and allowing your center of gravity to sink from your head down into your lower abdomen. Again, do not be put off by thinking that any of these strategies require great expertise or coaching. You already know how to do it—relaxed and content after a good meal, chilled in your favorite chair.

EXERCISE

EMBODIMENT AND CENTERING

Take a few minutes to be quiet.

Recall those times when you feel relaxed and content. Perhaps it happens for you after a good Sunday lunch. Perhaps on holiday. Sitting in your favorite café. Looking out across a beautiful view. On a park bench. After lovemaking. After exercise and movement.

In those situations you are physically comfortable and content. Sinking into yourself and calm.

Right now, see if you can allow yourself to sink into those same sensations.

Let your stomach sink and relax.

Lower your chin slightly.

Lower your eyes slightly as if looking down to the ground.

Notice the sensations on the soles of your feet.

Notice the sensations of your clothes on your thighs and your bottom.

Take three very slow, quiet, and calm deep breaths down into your abdomen.

Allow yourself to sink down into yourself, as if you were sinking into a good rest.

Explore sensing that you are connected with the earth beneath you. Gravity pulls you down. Your energy sinks down into the center of the earth.

You feel comfortable and chilled, just watching the world go by. Just like sitting at your favorite café or in your favorite chair or sofa or on a beach.

Content and watching the world go by.

CORE SKILL NO. 3: KIND AND WATCHFUL, THE INNER SMILE

The third core skill ensures that your mood and attitude do not sabotage your spiritual connection. In order to sense, guide, and deepen your spiritual connection, it is crucial that your mind be kind and friendly.

To repeat the crucial information shared above: your whole body, via your nervous and endocrine systems, is the organ that senses and experiences your spiritual connection. Your body, therefore, needs to be in the appropriate neuroendocrinologic state—the right mood—in order for you to sense your spiritual connection. If your body is in a state of anxiety or arousal, then you will not be able to register your spiritual connection because your major experience will be related to the anxiety or arousal.

If your mind is in a cold and alienated mood, it sends signals down into your neural and endocrine systems that reinforce and even initiate arousal and anxiety. It might be that your mind is often, or perhaps continuously, in an anxious or bad mood. If so, you are sabotaging your ability to feel spiritual connection. So you have to calm that anxiety.

A friendlier and warmer mental attitude is needed. A kind mind with good humor sends signals through your neuroendocrinologic system, relaxing tissue and making it much easier for you to feel your spiritual connection.

To put it another way, it is spiritually helpful if your own mood, frequency, and wavelength are similar to, or harmonic with, the frequency of the benevolent field. It makes it much easier to connect. A negative mental attitude creates "noise" that jams the external signal. The field is benevolent. If your mental attitude is not benevolent, it jams and blocks your ability to tune in and connect. The vibrations are incongruent.

If God is love, then the resonance of your own negative attitude may block you from feeling that love. If the Tao is a great ocean of benevolent vitality, then your own psychological stiffness may block you from the sensations and benefits of being in the flow. A kind and watchful mind allows and supports connection and flow.

I am not suggesting here that you just switch on a joyous, positive rapture that loves everyone and everything. I am, however, suggesting that you have to adopt an attitude that is kind and watchful, the compassionate witness. A relaxed attitude of goodwill.

Again, this attitude is similar to one you may have after a good meal or when you are in one of your favorite places, just sitting there, happy to watch the world pass by in front of you. Noticing, not judging. A mellowness in your thoughts and reflections and a philosophical good humor.

The skill, then, is to have a kind attitude to your own body, so that you can guide your good-humored and contented awareness so that it focuses down into your own body.

In many meditation traditions, giving kind attention to your own body is taught in an exercise known as the Inner Smile. It is a brilliant and simple exercise, and if I were able to recommend only one exercise in this book, it might be this one. The Inner Smile is explicitly inculcated in Taoist, tantric, and Buddhist meditation, but is also taught in a more symbolic and very alluring way in many other diverse spiritual cultures. All of these strategies teach you how to send kind messages through your neuroendocrinologic network, in order to help you be stable, open, and spiritually sensitive. These other traditions, including Christianity and paganism, use a variety of symbols, which you visualize as being located inside your own body. You will be familiar with many of them. They include

- pots, grails, cauldrons, and chalices;

- trees of life;

- inner worlds; and

- smiling wide-hipped gods and goddesses.

All of them, when located within your body, are metaphors for how your body needs your Inner Smile. The pots require that you fill them with a benevolent attitude, not toads' eyes and bats' wings. What will you stir into your chalice? You choose what moods and thoughts you place into the cauldron of your neuroendocrinologic system, your body. Will you stew in the poisons of negative emotions, thoughts, and attitudes? Or will you stew in the honey of kindness and understanding?

Fill your pot with negativity or alienation and it will be more difficult to feel your spiritual connection. Fill it with good things, milk, and honey, and the cauldron will simmer in a way that eases your connection.

Similarly, there is a tree of life growing inside you. You will find this metaphor in many spiritual traditions, such as Jewish Kabbala, and it is the key image in James George Frazer's famous study of magic and religion, *The Golden Bough*.[9] What does this tree need if it is to flourish and blossom and absorb the rays of the spiritual sun? It does not like inner moods of lightning, storms, or drought. Your inner tree of life needs a benevolent emotional and mental climate, friendly weather, and appropriate watering. Once more, the lesson is about the attitude you have to your body. It needs to be a kind and attentive relationship.

In other spiritual traditions whole worlds, landscapes, and star systems are placed in the cavern of our abdomens, and they too teach the same lesson. You may have seen these images in alchemy or Hinduism or the Aztec culture. These inner worlds require the blessing of their deity, and in this case their deity is your own consciousness. The attitude needed is that of a loving, not a wrathful, god. In the same way that the Creator loves the cosmos, so you too need to love your own internal world.

And then, of course, there are all the images of the smiling, wide-hipped goddesses and Buddhas with potbellies, always serene, never grimacing. They evoke an attitude and mood that is sweet, not sour. Imagine a chuckling Buddha sitting in your lower stomach. And Jesus at his most kind in your heart.

EXERCISE
THE INNER SMILE

When you are familiar with this technique, it is something you can do in a few seconds anywhere and anytime. You can also do it for a longer period as a form of self-healing and relaxation.

Pause.

Switch on an attitude of kindness and mental generosity.

Open your heart.

Soften your eyes.

Relax your stomach and breathe softly.

Turn your focus and attention down into your own body.

In the same way that you might lean down and care for an injured child or cradle an injured bird in your cupped hands, you direct this same quality of kind care down into your own body.

Have a kind and loving attitude toward your own body.

Especially where you may experience some distress, tension, or pain, direct your kind attitude directly into the tissue and allow yourself to be completely present to it, accepting, tolerant, and kind. Hold and cradle it.

Your attitude has the same care and interest as you might put into a craft or hobby such as embroidery or electronics—meticulous and calm. It also has the same compassion and affection as you would give to a beloved who is in distress.

If you want, you can envisage your body as being a large pot or cauldron or chalice—and your Inner Smile fills the container with benevolence.

If you want, you can envisage your body as being like a tree with a strong trunk and deep roots. Your Inner Smile is like the sun feeding the tree with light and warmth.

CORE SKILL NO. 4: YIELDING TO THE FEELING OF CONNECTION

The fourth core skill is that of being able to yield to the feelings and sensations of your spiritual connection. To let spirit into you. This is easy. It is just like relaxing in a warm bath.

You know what this is like. You come home from a tough day and get into the tub. The warm water feels good. You lie in it for a minute and then you could just get out of the bath quickly, having had an efficient and quick clean. On the other hand, as you will have experienced many times, you can choose to stay in the bath longer, relax, and surrender to the enjoyable sensation.

You make a choice to surrender to the good sensation and soak in it. You allow the good feeling to penetrate your body.

This is the skill—pausing and surrendering to the good feeling—that you need to transfer to the situations and circumstances in which you are spiritually connected. So there you are experiencing a moment of connection with the numinous. Instead of just letting it pass, you choose to give it more attention and to allow yourself a fuller and more mindful experience.

This is where the four skills combine and integrate.

- You pause and become mindful. You notice what is happening.

- You relax and center down into your body.

- You switch on your Inner Smile.

- You then notice the subtle, or perhaps obvious, sensations of a spiritual connection and you allow the experience to sink into you. You yield to the feeling.

You can see here how the first three skills—pausing and being mindful, being relaxed and embodied, and having a kind attitude—combine so that, when it is happening, you can be fully present to your spiritual experience. Then, fully present, fully aware of what is happening, you can cooperate with the spiritual experience, yield, and let it in. The Muslim poet Rumi described this yielding as dissolving like sugar. Addressing the great mystery of life and death, Rumi requested:

Chapter 2

Dissolver of sugar, dissolve me, if this is the time.
Do it gently with a touch of a hand, or a look.

Rumi's metaphor of dissolving is a good one and is similar to advice given in Taoist self-healing techniques. In order to fully absorb cosmic healing energy, you must yield and surrender with the softest and most featherlight of attitudes. As one experienced qi gung teacher said to me, "The softer, the deeper." In this way, it is possible to sense your spiritual connection gently sinking down deep into your bones and bone marrow.

Noticing the sensations and yielding to them may be a completely new skill for you, but, as we saw at the beginning of this section, it is not so different from allowing yourself to relax in a hot bath instead of getting out quickly. It is similar too to a massage, when you instinctively know you need to relax into the experience. Or perhaps you have been dragged, resistant, to a party or away for the day, and after a while you decide it is no good continuing to resist, but is time to surrender and enjoy the experience.

This surrender and yielding can also be enhanced by an attitude of acceptance, appreciation, and gratitude. The Christian mystic Meister Eckhart said, "If the only prayer you say in your life is *thank you*, that would suffice." This gratitude is a response to what you are receiving. The man leaning on the gate, looking at a beautiful landscape, felt gratitude for what he was experiencing and absorbed the experience more deeply.

EXERCISE
YIELDING TO THE EXPERIENCE

When you are relaxed, embodied, good-humored, and watchful, and in a situation that has connected you with the magic of life, be mindful of how your mood has changed and how your experience has altered.

Inside this new mood, notice the sensations and feelings within you that come from your spiritual connection.

Be careful not to tense up or become too focused or earnest. Just allow yourself to slip into a more receptive state. Yield and surrender to the experience.

Allow the sensations of your spiritual connection to penetrate and permeate your body. Be like a sponge absorbing warm water.

If it feels appropriate and authentic, express appreciation and gratitude. "Thank you, life. Thank you, spirit. Thank you, cosmos."

Perhaps this moment of connection lasts only a few seconds.

Perhaps you soak in it for a while. Or even for a lifetime.

PLANNING YOUR SPIRITUAL PRACTICE

Your relationship with the wonder and energy, your rapport with "God," develops and deepens over time. You build a greater intimacy and familiarity in the same way that you develop a relationship with a friend or pet or place. You simply have to spend more time with them in order to know them better. And the more time you spend hanging out and dwelling in this rapport with the numinous, the more you support the development of your heart and consciousness.

It may be similar, for instance, to your relationship with music. If you love music, you spend time with it in situations in which you are not distracted by other noises and events.

So the more you pause and allow yourself to dwell in the experience of your spirituality, the more you will become accustomed to it and familiar with it, continuously sensing its presence, subtle but supportive.

You might want me to advise you about what gateways and circumstances will be best for you, but I have to reply that I do not know because I am not inside your skin, and you are the greatest expert on yourself. You might also want me to advise you on what time of day and for how long you should do your connecting, and, again, I would have to reply, I do not know. One second of connection, touched, for example, by the beauty of the sky, is worthwhile. A lifetime of continuous connection with the wonder and energy, humming permanently and soaking into every cell of your being, is better.

Nevertheless, if you push me to be a prescriptive guru, I urge you minimally to take some time at least once a day to enjoy your connection and plug into your natural and cosmic environment. A few minutes is worthwhile but, of course, the longer the better. Ultimately you want an ongoing experience, and it is persistent daily practice that will set up the deep grooves of an embedded habit, which will also carry you through tough times.

I also suggest that you plan a calendar in which you deliberately place yourself in those circumstances you know are particularly good for you and help you soak up and fully absorb your connection. These are top-ups and reinforcements. They might be special trips into landscape or to art galleries, or group meditation or music or massage or church or pilgrimage, and so on.

If possible, too, find a friend or group of friends with whom you can share relaxed conversations about spirituality. It is not just that there are psychological benefits from having the support and solidarity of companions. There is also a helpful ambience and connection that happens when friends talk together about spirituality. In Hinduism this is called *satsang*. In the West, Jesus spoke of it as "when two or more are gathered."

PLANNING YOUR SPIRITUAL PRACTICE

It may help you to have a chart that plans your spiritual practice.

Daily

1. This is what I can easily do every day to connect . . .

2. This is when and where I will do it . . .

3. I will do it for this long . . .

Top-Ups

1. These are the circumstances and situations that will inspire and support my spirituality and that I can do occasionally . . .

2. This is when and where I will do them . . .

3. I will do them for this long . . .

DUVET SPIRITUALITY AND OTHER HEALTH BENEFITS

Connection with the wonder and energy. *Joie de vivre.* The growth of compassion and awareness. These are wonderful things. They are also very personal and very private, and their growth can happen even when we are in situations of great distress. In fact, in the next chapter we will look at how crises and illness can be enormously redemptive opportunities for spiritual growth.

This is such a crucial point. The development of our spirituality is not dependent on the success and comfort of our external circumstances. One of the best examples of this is what I call "duvet spirituality."

Chapter 2

DUVET SPIRITUALITY

Imagine that you have had an awful day at work or with the family. You have had enough of them all! Rather than rant or dump your mood on anyone else, you sensibly choose to disappear under your duvet. Grumbling and perhaps even resentful, you plonk yourself in bed or on a sofa. You simmer for a while and then begin to sink into the beginnings of a rest.

You have withdrawn from all the work and family problems and are now alone, sunk into yourself. There are some metaphors here that might now be appropriate for your state: you are like a seed in the earth; you are like an infant in the womb; you have taken sensible spiritual retreat.

Then, within the privacy of your duvet retreat, you can practice your spiritual connection. You slowly switch on your Inner Smile and give kind and accepting attention to yourself.

You then allow yourself to become aware of the natural world and the cosmos. Whatever your mood, nature and wonder are still there.

You allow yourself to feel your spiritual connection and you let it in.

In this way, you have surfed your overwhelmed and unhappy mood and guided yourself into spiritual experience.

This exercise demonstrates clearly how your spiritual development—the growth of your connection, heart, and mindfulness—is not dependent upon external circumstances. Your spirituality stands sovereign and independent of your external state of affairs. It just needs you to come home to yourself and withdraw from the stimulation of the world. Retreat is not done only in monasteries and in mountains. It is an attitude of knowing when to withdraw into yourself.

All of this goes some way to answering the riddle posed in the very opening pages of this book, which asked what it was about religion and spirituality that improved people's lives. It is an interior activity that continues regardless of work, family, and health, and, restating the obvious, it is good for you because it benefits your general sense of well-being to connect regularly with the wonder of life. It just feels good. This obviously spills over into generally supporting your emotional and psychological health.

Second, this spiritual connection can be sustained and developed regardless of what is going on in the rest of your life. At worst, your life could be chaotic and challenging, but nevertheless this does not need to cut across your spirituality. Spirituality gives you independence in the management of your psychological well-being. It provides an enduring core to your life, whatever else you have to manage.

This could be particularly helpful when, for example, you might be passing through a period in which you are lacking confidence. Connection with the cosmos is more powerful and inspiring than anything else. I remember one woman, a nurse, who suffered from low self-esteem and was continually striving to meet other people's expectations. But she also had a heart of gold. As she developed her skills of spiritual connection, she realized she had a good rapport with the wonder and energy, which was often deepened when she was with particular patients, with her family, or listening to music and in nature. As she realized all this, her low self-esteem simply dissolved. She knew now that she had nothing to prove to anyone and that she was part of a wondrous universe.

To practice the core skills of pausing, centering, and connecting, regardless of your circumstances, is both psychologically empowering and hugely beneficial for your physical health because, obviously, these strategies are huge stress reducers and enablers of relaxation. I would go so far as to suggest too that there is no greater health-giving relaxation than the "swoon" you might feel when yielding to the beauty of spiritual connection. There is no deeper method for opening up your tissue, improving flexibility and flow, and building a strong immune system.

At the same time, from a more metaphysical perspective and following Asian medical traditions, as you experience your spiritual connection you simultaneously open up and absorb health-giving vitality—*prana*, *qi*. This is a double-wave of physical benefits: your tissue becomes more open and fluid, and simultaneously you absorb vitality. This is surely the foundation of great health.[10]

Moreover, your increased sense of well-being and self-management will almost certainly spill over into a general psychological attitude that is generally more upbeat, optimistic, and supportive of other people. You become a better and more enjoyable person to have around. Your increased inner well-being creates an ambience that enhances the lives of others.

In my own life, my ongoing and deepening spiritual connection has thawed my old harshness and helped me become more conscious and loving.

I think too of another friend, another man whose character was filled with cold anger, but whose spiritual development has transformed him. He gets his spiritual connection mainly through nature and landscape, but he also lies in bed at night counting his blessings and letting himself be touched by the magic of life, especially the magic of his young children. Over the years I have watched a closed, highly strung, and aggressive character steadily melt into a compassionate and thoughtful friend, colleague, and father.

These examples are in many ways the proof of the endeavor. Spiritual connection changes us. But we are only too human and can be difficult and resistant to change, can't we? So our spirituality also requires careful reflection and self-management, which is the focus of the next chapters.

Part Two

REFLECTION

CHAPTER 3

AWAKENING AND SELF-MANAGEMENT

✳

The vision of personal spiritual development is a high ideal. It goes far beyond the usual goals for a happy and materially successful life with status, satisfying relationships, and good health. The ambition is that we grow into men and women who are continuously conscious of our connection with spirit and continuously awake, compassionate, and connected.

This fulfillment of our potential is a natural outcome of being part of the wonder and energy of creation. Connected to the great ocean of beneficence, how can we possibly not develop into something more wonderful? In the way that seeds expand into great trees and mysterious cosmic events emerge into galaxies, so we too are emergent and developmental beings.

But, in striving toward this high ideal, we need to be careful. On one side we have the love, benevolence, and wisdom that come from our connection with the spirit of life. On the other side, though, we have the realities of being human, and we all know only too well that being human is not easy.

In this part of the book I want to explore how we can guide ourselves into a state of greater connection, compassion, and consciousness, while at the same time being realistic about the possible challenges. In this chapter we look at the core strategies of reflection and self-management. Then, in the next, we explore the difficulties we may face and how best to guide and relieve them.

THE PARADOX AND POIGNANCY

This whole subject is full of paradox and poignancy, and spirituality is sometimes a difficult balance. As a teacher and author I often feel conflicted: on one hand, I want to inspire and encourage people about their innate goodness and the wonder of creation; on the other hand, I do not want to support naïveté about the human condition. We are magnificent beings with cosmic consciousness, and yet at the same time we are also insecure and can do harm. I find this paradox very poignant, and it is recognized as a reality by all wise spirituality.

In one of my workshops on the psychology of spiritual development, a woman once came up to me and complained that I was not cheering her up and helping her to connect with spirit. "Why can't this be like your other workshops, when I feel inspired and connected to all the joy and energy? This is all so gloomy," she complained.

Her criticism saddened me and I paused to spend time with her and listen more carefully. A few minutes later, she shared with me that she had suffered from depression for most of her life and that a loved one had recently died.

And here we have it in a single poignant situation: a human being who is connected to the wonder of creation and yet simultaneously melancholy.

Being realistic, we all of us, in one way or another, contain these contradictions, and spiritual growth cannot progress fruitfully and achieve its fulfillment unless we address these realities. That woman's melancholy cannot be ignored, not if she is to grow into full spiritual happiness. With wisdom and care, her melancholy needs to be met, healed, and integrated, or else it will continue as an unwelcome guest.

All of this points out why it is so important that we take conscious and compassionate responsibility for ourselves. This is precisely why we find the practice of self-reflection at the heart of all spiritual traditions.

THE ELEMENTS OF SELF-REFLECTION

Because self-reflection is such an important strategy for self-development, its usefulness is also fully recognized not just in spirituality but also in education, therapy, social work, human resources, and the caring professions. "Witness consciousness" is considered to be a necessary and very useful part of professional development and a successful career. In fact, reflective self-auditing is built into the statutory job descriptions for many of these professions. Head teachers in England, for example, are supposed to have thirty minutes' reflective practice built into the timetable of their working week. Indeed, in a 2009 survey of UK head teachers, "a need for more time and opportunities for reflection" pervaded their responses.[1]

This professional use of self-reflection for personal growth and to improve performance is an inspiring convergence of spiritual and secular practice, and I have put together three summaries that I hope you find helpful.

Reflection is our ability to

- look at ourselves and our willingness to learn more about who we really are, the nature of our character and psychology, our real purpose and essence;

- observe, inquire into, and contemplate ourselves, our thoughts, our emotions, and our instincts; play back memories and impressions locked within the subconscious, meeting them, endeavoring to understand, accept, and integrate them; anticipate our future and how our past may influence it; and

- use our higher consciousness, our reasoning mind, to observe, review, examine, and judge our thoughts and behavior and contemplate the larger order of nature; listen to the inner voice of our wiser self; not blame others but understand that we can create our own lives and consciously change ourselves; and keep an open mind.

All of these are important prompts to switch on our most careful intelligence and wisdom. This is the same kind of intelligence, care, and intuition that we might use when helping a good friend explore important life choices; except here we are using this quality of intelligence on ourselves.

This ability to observe and reflect on our own lives, as if we were detached witnesses, is one of the core themes of spirituality. Do not be unconscious. Do not sleepwalk through life. Wake up. Wake up from the trance of habit. Wake up and be aware of what is really happening and how you really are.

It is worth recalling that, traditionally, great spiritual connection always goes hand in hand with deep wisdom, psychological insight, and compassion.

Dissatisfaction Wakes Us Up

We are all of us caught in this paradoxical wrestle between how we are now and how we feel we might be. We have a sense and instinct for how we can grow, and at the same time we experience who we are right now. There is an instinct to develop. Just as if someone tries to suffocate you, your life force will explode so that you can breathe, so we also possess a powerful drive to liberate ourselves from the suffocation of being less than we truly are.

There is a natural dynamic within us that seeks to free us from anything that imprisons us, not just from external offenders, but also from our own restrictive emotions, attitudes, and thoughts. This dynamic is the grit of awakening and self-betterment. It is dissatisfaction that often prods us into a reflective space where we know that we cannot just stay the way that we are. We need to shift. It is famous that within classical Chinese there is no equivalent of the word *crisis*. There is only a glyph that translates as "a good opportunity to make a decision." This ancient concept is spiritual wisdom: there are no crises, only opportunities for change.

Without movement, expansion, and growth, we stagnate, which leads to physical and psychological discomfort. Many of us, however, may spend many years ignoring, denying, or quick-fixing this irritability, anaesthetizing it with alcohol, consumerism, status competition, tribalism, and other habits and compulsions, or just stoically repressing it; and others of us may just stay stuck, feeling as if our lives are boring and without meaning. Even if you achieve ongoing success at work and at home, you may still ache for something more meaningful.

I have watched friends enjoying decades of material comfort, success, and status, and during that time they have not changed or grown. Their cultural and work skills may have improved as part of their professional development, but emotionally and spiritually they were static. But once they had been thrown a curveball of dangerous illness or family tragedy, something deep within began to shift, and true development started.

Recognizing how the heart opens and consciousness wakes up during periods of stress and crisis, some spiritual traditions actually developed fast-track techniques of discomfort and tension to trigger spiritual awakening. You will find fasting and long periods of isolation in most traditions, including Christianity, Islam, and Buddhism. There are also strategies of extreme asceticism, which you will also find in most traditions, but they are often associated with the yogis of Hinduism. There are also strategies of repeated actions, such as a prayer or a gesture or a mantra, done for very long periods of time, which you will also find all over the world and which help seekers to alter their consciousness and break free of their usual psychological and social conditioning.

I do not recommend any of these approaches, but I nevertheless feel a certain admiration for those souls who throw themselves into extreme situations in order to be liberated. Most people, I find, do not require these radical stimulations. Daily life is sufficiently formidable.

THE ABILITY TO EXAMINE YOUR OWN LIFE IS NATURAL

One of my own pivotal life decisions was to leave teaching in a university in order to work in a deprived inner-city area with students with learning difficulties. Teaching at the London School of Economics was intellectually stimulating, but I felt this arena of academic competitiveness was not good for developing my heart, so I made a careful decision to move to Southwark College, where I stayed for a decade, mainly tutoring drop-in sessions for men and women of any age, sixteen upward, many with special needs, who had missed out on their schooling and wanted to come back into education. These sessions brought them up to speed with their literacy and numeracy skills, built their confidence and self-esteem, and helped to clarify their next steps.

For most of these students, their early experience of education had been disastrous, usually because of harsh and dysfunctional homes or because of their own disruptive and antisocial behavior. Many came from environments as dangerous, cruel, and marginalized as you will find anywhere. Some were refugees who had endured rape and torture. Many of the women were single parents, and many of them had hostile partners who criticized, demeaned, and beat them.

Their courage and determination were inspiring, particularly their powerful instinct to move forward and create new lives for themselves and their children. Sometimes I saw students only once or twice. Others came for a couple of years until they felt able to move on with confidence. The most important thing I learned during those years was that, given a safe and friendly space, with a respectful attitude, people develop and grow.

Living in an ostentatiously rich city like London, these men and women were only too aware of where they stood in the social pecking order and how poverty deprived them and their children of the opportunities and access enjoyed by the majority of other Londoners.

These adult students, voluntarily choosing to come back into education, had woken up. They understood how their backgrounds had made them what they were and how their own current attitudes and mindset affected them, their families, and their life chances. They knew they had to develop and reach beyond their social circumstances and conditioning. They had a deep sense that they could do better and be better. They were very self-aware about what they were doing and why they were doing it.

In the midst of oppressive social circumstances, their spirits had woken up and transcended their psychological, social, and material situations. They were able to look at themselves. This ability to step back and watch yourself is a form of enlightenment. It is a crucial part of spiritual awakening and self-management. Here, for me, is one of the wonders of being human, that you can step outside your story and watch it as if watching a movie. This is a sign of a very sophisticated brain and nervous system, and you are using it right now as you read this book and can think about yourself reading it.

These words *enlightenment* and *spiritual awakening* are sometimes associated with a spiritual elite, but they belong to all of us and are a hardwired part of our makeup. Your mind, your consciousness, is capable of this detachment, this witnessing and observing of yourself.

But this detachment and witnessing is a spiritual muscle that needs to be exercised and strengthened. The ability is there in all of us. The goal is to have it switched on all the time, permanently. And then it is not just a cold and distant watchfulness, but it is done with an ambience of compassion, wisdom, and understanding. Always watching. Always loving.

Chapter 3

INTRODUCING REFLECTION

Pause for a few moments.

Recall a time in your life when you were not satisfied with yourself or with your circumstances.

This may have been associated with a relationship or your health or your work or with wanting to live somewhere new.

Do you remember spending some time thinking about it and pondering what you might do next? Do you recall weighing up different options?

Recognize that when you were weighing up those different options, you were in a space of contemplation and reflection.

Do you remember a time when you had behaved badly and afterward you were thinking about it, regretting it, and wondering how you might make things better?

You were then, too, in a space of reflection.

Notice that to be calm and detached, watching yourself, contemplating what you have done and what you might do, is natural.

In the midst of life's ongoing challenges, this is one of the most beautiful miracles of the human psyche—this drive we have, fuelled by the life force, to wake up and look, with reason and thoughtfulness, at our own lives. We all of us have this ability to back off from our lives, create some mental distance, and look at our own behavior, emotions, and even our way of thinking.

For Plato, this ability to reason—to be reasonable and to think things through—was one of the proofs of the human soul. We can be insecure and aggressive, addictive and compulsive, but we are also capable of calm reflection and intelligent decision making. We naked apes have such evolved brains and minds that we can watch our own lives, even our own thoughts.

Self-Reflection at Any Age and in Any Situation

It is beautiful to watch young children pausing to consider their actions. This is one of the major goals, for example, of a classroom method called Circle Time, which is used in many UK primary schools and can be found in different forms across the world. In a safe and calm ambience, young children are guided to consider their behavior, its consequences, and the feelings of other children.[2] In these situations I have heard children say things like, "I hurt his feelings, made him feel bad, when I pushed him. I'm sorry. I won't do it again"; "She's sad today, so I'll be kind"; "I could be better"; "Maybe I could share my toys more."

I saw self-reflection, too, being impeccably modeled by my friend Eileen Caddy, right up until her death at the age of eighty-nine. A spiritual teacher and best-selling author, Eileen practiced what she preached.[3] Every morning, usually before dawn, she sat for at least an hour's meditation. In the silence, she connected deeply and soaked in what she was happy to call unconditional love. At the same time, with a compassionate and observant mind, she would scan her feelings, her thoughts, and her behavior over the previous day.

"There's always something to work on," she would say. "Always something that is out of tune with unconditional love. I work on myself. I let God work on me. I'm a piece of work," she laughed.

Her life had been informed and driven by spiritual practice and service, but she had been in two marriages and there had been challenges with her relationships and family. She was also the cofounder of the Findhorn Foundation in Scotland, a spiritual community that pioneered the integration of multifaith, ecological, and psychological awareness. In her meditation she always reflected on how she was managing these relationships, noticing where she had lost her tolerance and affection and where she needed to be more forgiving, supportive, and loving; noticing, too, her vulnerability and her tendency to misperceive what people felt about her.

With her heart open and her mind compassionate, she looked at her shadow and negative patterns. She was brutally honest with herself, but it never slipped into a destructive remorse, shame, or guilt. She always knew that she was part of a benevolent and loving cosmos.

Even in her final years, when she was frail and occasionally racked with spinal pain, she could joke that her desire for death was just a way of avoiding her current lesson. She saw clearly what she still had to learn. Stoic and proud, she realized that she needed to allow herself to receive help. She needed to learn how to receive and accept the humility of being feeble—accepting it all, not in an embarrassed or begrudging way, but with love and genuine gratitude. Her reflection and willingness to understand and learn her next lesson were faultless.

In this vein I am always amused and touched by this deepest of reflective prayers, whose source, as far as I have been able to ascertain, is unknown, although it is frequently quoted on websites:

Dear God,
So far today, I've done all right.
I haven't gossiped.
I haven't lost my temper.
I haven't been greedy, grumpy, nasty, selfish, or overindulgent.
I'm very thankful for that.
But in a few minutes, God, I'm going to get out of bed and from then on, I'm probably going to need a lot more help.
Amen.

BEING HONEST WITH OURSELVES

All traditions and cultures that honor education and personal development possess a clear understanding that we need consistent and regular reflective practice, conducted in an attitude of safe retreat, in which we pause, detach, and assess where we are and then make decisions about how best to guide our next steps. Think of any monastery, convent, abbey, or college at Oxford or Cambridge, and picture the cloisters. These covered walkways around a quiet garden were designed for contemplation and reflection. At the very heart of Buddhist practice is meditation, with its inherent self-reflection.

Socrates famously asserted that the unexamined life was not worth living. Even Norman Vincent Peale, who founded the influential American positive-thinking movement, which normally advises people to gloss over negativity and focus only on the positive, said, "One of the greatest moments in anybody's developing experience is when he no longer tries to hide from himself but determines to get acquainted with himself as he really is."

In spiritual development, this leads to these kinds of questions:

- How well am I connecting with the wonder and energy of life?

- Are my heart and consciousness growing? Am I kind enough? Watchful enough?

- What new insights do I have about myself and my state?

- Am I being of service to the community of life?

- Am I supporting the spiritual development of my spouse, family, and friends?

- What kind of vibration and ambience do I radiate toward my family, friends, and colleagues?

- What is blocking me? What do I need now to take myself forward?

In the most classic daily exercise of spiritual self-reflection, you pause and slowly survey the previous twenty-four hours. As you scan through the day, you look with honesty at your behavior and attitudes. You assess your levels of kindness and mindfulness, especially with those closest to you.

The challenge is to practice self-examination without either fooling or punishing yourself. To avoid delusion, there is a reflective tool used in human-resources management called a *three-hundred-and-sixty-degree feedback process*, also known as *multisource assessment*. In this process, all your colleagues, regardless of their status, give feedback on your attitude, talents, and behavior. Can you imagine receiving realistic feedback from everyone you know, including your family?

But in a parallel piece of research it was shown that the least reliable feedback came from colleagues who had known the subject for more than five years and, through familiarity, had lost their ability to assess realistically.[4] This is a caution to us. We have all known ourselves for longer than five years and are subject to self-delusion.

For this reason, self-reflection needs to be done with some care and intelligence. I frequently hear from students and colleagues that they do their self-reflection as part of their ongoing lifestyle, noticing minute by minute their behavior and attitudes. I admire this, but what is also needed is a regular practice that is more considered, thoughtful, and penetrating.

Especially in dark times, journal keeping too can be a sustainable way of reflecting on yourself. Henri Nouwen, for example, was a Catholic priest, author, and spiritual director who later in his life suffered a particularly difficult period but found sustenance in his journal. "To my surprise," he wrote, "I never lost the ability to write. In fact, writing became part of my struggle for survival. It gave me the little distance from myself that I needed to keep from drowning in my despair."[5]

RECALLING THE PREVIOUS TWENTY-FOUR HOURS—AND COMPASSIONATE EQUANIMITY

Pause and let yourself settle down comfortably.

Take your mind back twenty-four hours and remember where you were and what you were doing.

Then slowly allow your memory to roll forward, remembering what you were doing.

In particular, recall your mood. What quality of emotion and attitude were you carrying and communicating to others?

In your interactions with other people, were you positive or negative? What was your agenda?

Just notice these things.

If you behaved well and positively, be sure to notice it.

If you were less than loving, notice this too. You may feel some remorse and a wish to behave differently next time.

Contemplate the meaning of the phrase "compassionate equanimity"— detached and philosophical, but empathic and loving.

Have compassionate equanimity toward yourself in all things.

Just noticing and being aware of a problematic attitude can be enough to change it. If, for example, day by day you pause to look at your behavior and keep noticing that your attitude to someone is unkind, there is a strong likelihood that you will stop it. Just having it in your awareness can be enough to shift you.

The difficulty with negative attitudes and behaviors is that you may often deny or ignore their very existence. But, in honest self-reflection, sooner or later you face and own up to your stuff. This act of acknowledgement and ownership is often 90 percent of transformation. In psychotherapy it is well known that change can come only after people have admitted they have a problem. It is like standing in the road and seeing a car coming at you—you get out of the way. Movement is natural.

LEARNING FROM OUR LIFE EXPERIENCE WHEREVER WE ARE

I also watched a diligent practice of self-reflection similar to Eileen Caddy's in a young man, Mike, who found a deep nurture and balance in his daily reflection. He was a successful entrepreneur and had made his first millions, but his life was full of the usual pressures, chaos, and stimulation—a full-on job, a partner struggling with having just become a mother, and a baby who liked to stay up all night.

His career needed attention. His relationship was strained. Being a parent was exhausting. But, on his way home from work every day, he would stop in his car for ten minutes to pause, connect, and review his life. He looked at his behavior and attitudes and asked the basic questions: Am I becoming more awake and loving? Am I growing? Am I of service? What do I need to develop?

He placed his work and family life within this framework of spiritual reflection, and this brought a coherence and peace of mind.

Here you can perceive the profound benefits of self-reflection. In particular, it puts the brakes on agitated and ingrained patterns of behavior. It throws light on attitudes that, if left unnoticed, can persistently sabotage not just your spiritual growth, but also your work and relationships.

In his daily reflection, for example, Mike had to acknowledge the feedback he often received that his sense of humor was frequently inappropriate and hurtful. When people, especially his wife, accused him of this, he would become defensive or even cockier, brushing off their criticism as unwarranted and saying they simply did not share his sense of humor.

In self-reflection, however, he had no choice but to look at their feedback and hear what they said. He could see that he was being too sharp and hurtful, and that he did indeed need to stop doing it. But, at the same time, he also reflected on why he did it and noticed that, in particular, he was sharp when he was either tired or under attack. He realized, therefore, that he needed also to manage his fatigue and look at his patterns of defensiveness.

Again, to some people this may all seem to be too introspective, but from the perspective of Mike's wife and his colleagues, it was obviously valuable and positive.

This form of self-managed development belongs to all of us, wherever we are, whoever we are.

REVISITING THE FOUR CORE SKILLS

In practicing self-reflection you need the same four core skills you use to deepen your spiritual connection:

- pause and be mindful;

- be relaxed, centered, and grounded in your body;

- observe what is happening in a kind and good-humored way;

- yield to the feeling of connection.

Eileen Caddy's self-reflective practice exemplified these. She paused in meditation. She always grounded softly into her body. Her attitude toward herself was kind and observant. She was also aware of the subtle feeling of being connected to God and constantly yielding to it. Mike also demonstrated this process of reflection, pausing in his car, settling into the car seat, watching himself with compassionate equanimity, and allowing his body to relax and connect.

It is worth spelling out why these skills are so necessary.

Pause and Be Mindful

It is difficult to practice self-reflection when you are in an agitated state of impatience or anxiety. This state is fuelled by the anxiety hormones, adrenaline and cortisol, and it is a well-documented psychological theory that it is very difficult to think clearly and make good decisions when in a condition of arousal, driven by the biological instincts of fright, fight, or flight. Clear and intelligent reflection comes from a considered state, not from agitation.[6]

So you will need to assess when it is easiest for you to pause, be calm, and be mindful. It might be in sitting meditation or working on a hobby or walking or having the television on in the background or sitting in the garden with a drink or after aerobic exercise, and so on. You use the circumstances that you know are the easiest for you.

I once supported a school principal who was having real difficulty finding the time and the right attitude to do reflective practice. We talked and uncovered that he relaxed most easily into a connected state when he was in his garage working on the engine of his classic car. We therefore agreed that he would take more time in his garage—not a hardship—and, while tinkering, would think in a calm and reflective way about his style of work, how he related and communicated, and how he might improve.

Be Relaxed, Centered and Grounded in Your Body

It is important to sink into and be comfortable in your body because it keeps you grounded and present. Some of you, when facing up to difficult issues, may have a habit of avoiding these harsh realities by slipping off into a kind of daydream. This is especially understandable if you have a painful personal history, in which going off into a daydream may well have been your best survival mechanism.

Sinking down into your body, relaxing, and calming your breath all help to stabilize and focus you, so that you have a serene and stable foundation from which you can look honestly at yourself.

I have tutored many people who carry the traumas of abusive childhoods and frightening illnesses. One woman stands out for me. She was recovering from intensive and very painful treatment for cancer of the throat and was very anxious and hardly able to be calm or reflective about herself and her situation. Slowly and carefully, I led her through the exercise of sinking down into her body, helping her to recall those situations when she did it naturally, such as after a good meal or in a sun chair by the pool.

"When I sank into my body, it felt so reassuring and safe," she said afterward. "For the first time in years, I was able to look clearly at everything that was going on in me. I could even face my fear. It was a great step forward for me."

Observing in a Kind and Good-Humored Way

It is also necessary to practice self-reflection as if you were the kindest person in the world looking after a beloved friend. In this case, the beloved friend is you. Introspection must be done with warm and philosophical good humor, with the Inner Smile, the strategy described earlier in the book, of focusing on your own body and feelings with an attitude of care and affection.

If it is done with a cold or judgmental attitude, your negative attitude will send harsh messages through your neuroendocrinologic system, creating sensations of anxiety and freezing you out of your connection with spirit.

Surrender to the Feeling of the Experience

This ability to watch yourself in a good-humored way—your kind watchfulness—must also be complemented by a *felt* experience of your connection to the benevolent hum of life. Your Inner Smile, focusing kindly on your own body and feelings, and your connection need to be tangibly experienced, so you feel genuinely supported by your contact with spirit.

Because self-reflection requires us to look at our shadows, negative aspects, and wounds, without a connected and kind attitude we might find ourselves lost in depression, shame, and self-punishing guilt. It is within the context of a benevolent cosmos, mediated by your kind and compassionate mind, that you can face your history and embrace it with an attitude that heals and integrates.

For a while I worked pastorally with a prisoner who was jailed for life, exploring the possibility of deep self-reflection on what he had done. Conversation would take us only so far. It was only when we meditated together and went into an atmosphere that was tangibly connected and compassionate that he could begin to manage his shame and confusion, develop some insight, and fully face the realities of his actions.

MEDITATION IS SOMETHING WE ALL DO

Why make things difficult? If we pull together the different skills and exercises described so far in this book, we shall find that we have arrived at the essence of meditation. I have practiced meditation for over forty years and have made a point of sitting in and experiencing as many of the different meditation schools as possible. I have been teaching it for several decades too, and I dare to say I have as full a modern knowledge of it as anyone. I have also listened and watched very carefully to see what enables people most easily to practice meditation.

I had one friend, for example, who claimed that trying to learn meditation was so stressful for him that all he got from it was a stomach ulcer. One day, however, when we were staying at the same center, I went to his room and found him sitting cross-legged on his bed, his back against the wall. He looked like a smiling Buddha. I asked him later what he had been doing. "Chilling for a while," he replied. "Just thinking about this and that. Watching my thoughts. Watching my feelings."

I was amused. He was sitting quietly for an extended period, in a state of relaxation, and noticing what was happening. He was meditating! But, when he had been in a formal class, *attempting* to meditate, it had only caused him stress.

Meditation is a natural human activity, which you probably already do although you may not know you are doing it. When you are relaxed and comfortable in your body—this might be after a good meal or sitting at your favorite café or looking across at the sea—you then just sit there in good humor watching the world go by. This is a form of meditation—calm and watching.

In "proper" meditation the only difference is that you are conscious and self-aware about the fact that you are meditating. You know what you are doing. You are awake to the fact that you are sitting there, watching with good humor. Moreover, you may *choose* to sit there or stay in that benevolently watchful state for a longer period of time.

In my opinion and experience, the key is to just sink into that comfortable and watchful state. Relaxed and awake. Do not be aroused or disturbed by any ideas you have that meditation is a discipline or difficult. Do not tense up as if you were being examined. Those are just echoes, in my opinion, of bad teaching, often deriving from martial-arts practices or a militaristic attitude to spirituality.

The key is to remain chilled, as if you were watching a satisfying movie or listening to beautiful music. This is how I like to teach meditation. It is something that you do already, only no one has ever told you so. When you are relaxed, embodied, and watching the world go by with good humor, you are in a natural state of contemplation and meditation.

EXERCISE
NATURAL MEDITATION

Sit or lie anywhere and in any position.

Check that your posture is comfortable.

Close your eyes and be aware that you want to sink into an ambience that is relaxed, calm, and watchful.

Also be aware that it may take a while to sink into that space and that you need to be patient.

If it feels comfortable, place your hands on your lower stomach. This helps to calm your body.

Allow your stomach to relax and sink.

Lower your chin slightly, as if looking down into your own body. This may also help to relax you, as it is part of the body language of relaxation.

Notice the rise and fall of your breath.

Your only task right now is just to watch and be patient.

All kinds of thoughts and feelings may arise in you. They are all, whatever they are, acceptable. Just be patient.

When you feel it is appropriate, begin to guide your attitude into the Inner Smile, so that it is kind, compassionate, and philosophical.

Open your heart.

Soften your eyes.

Adopt a kind mind.

Keep your stomach relaxed.

Take a few long, slow, and quiet breaths down into your abdomen.

Just continue to sit there, expecting nothing, just watching, in the same ambience as when you are normally content, good-humored, and observing.

If you start to feel agitated, soften your stomach, check your Inner Smile, and see whether watching the sensations of your breath is helpful. Be patient.

In the calm, you will be able to notice that you exist in this ongoing background hum of connection with the cosmic benevolence. Yield to this sensation and enjoy it.

Stay watching. Stay relaxed.

Stay there for a few minutes—or for a lifetime.

Someone who is very experienced at sinking into this space can meditate anywhere. You could be at Piccadilly Circus or in the queue from hell in a supermarket and you can nevertheless sink into your body, connect, and watch what is going on with compassionate equanimity. And the more times you do it, the easier it will become.

Sometimes if you are living a life full of speed, its agitation will spill over into your quiet times and calming down will take a while. Even with my decades of practice there are times when it may take thirty minutes of just sitting and watching before I slip into the calm zone.

It is in this meditation space, soaking comfortably in your connection, that your compassionate and inquiring mind can contemplate the meaning of life. You can arrive at your own insights and wisdom about the greatest mysteries of existence and the nature of consciousness.

TAKING REFLECTIVE TIME FOR SELF-HEALING

If, as a beginner, you tried to meditate on Saturday night in Piccadilly Circus in a crowded bar, you might find it difficult. The noise and atmosphere would be irritating and distracting. You would sit down, close your eyes, and probably start to feel uncomfortable. All the external stimuli would trigger irritable responses.

If, however, you are an experienced meditator, then all these stimuli would not affect you and your chemistry. Your hormones of arousal would not be stirred up and you could remain calm, because you are accustomed and habituated to the goads. You would notice and be aware of the provocative circumstances, but you would not react. You would remain in a state of equanimity.

This ability to stay calm and ignore stimulation is a key feature of meditation, and it is also precisely what you need to do when you feel your own thoughts and emotions rising to irritate and arouse you.

You carry your history and your condition in your psychology and in the cellular memory of your body, so when you sit still for extended periods it is possible that you will start to feel and think things that are usually repressed and below your normal threshold of consciousness. For example, you may have been sitting on some stress for several months, but nevertheless stoically getting on with your life. When you sit down to relax and meditate, therefore, instead of relaxing, what happens is that you begin to feel these previously ignored stress levels. Sometimes these thoughts and emotions may be worse than Piccadilly Circus. Sometimes they will be just mildly irritating, but enough to make you feel uncomfortable and want to avoid them by getting up, walking away, and distracting yourself with something else.

In the meditation traditions of Vipassana and Zen, practitioners are taught to just breathe and witness what is happening inside themselves, for many hours a day and for many years. Sooner or later, these traditions teach, every type of emotion and thought that is within you will arise from deep within the history of your psychology. Endless compassionate watchfulness and a calm breath, however, will ultimately melt and evaporate all these sensations and thoughts, until finally you are in a state of pure, connected mindfulness and consciousness.

Then there are other more active forms of meditation in which you deliberately engage with your psychological stuff in order to heal and integrate it. The essence of these techniques is that you stay connected and embodied and maintain the Inner Smile, as you give accepting and compassionate attention to whatever arises in you. Like a wonderful doctor and healer, you come into relationship with your internal stuff. And when you begin to experience any feelings of impatience or irritability—which are normal for everyone—you do not immediately get up in order to avoid them. Instead, as they arise, you stay watching them and accepting them with a benevolent ambience.

This is profound therapy, because you are fully present to the irritating sensations of negative and wounded patterns within you, but, instead of avoiding or repressing them, you give them accepting awareness. In psychological jargon, it is a form of catharsis as you reexperience past pain and allow it to shift. This awareness of your feelings and working constructively with them is the essence of *emotional literacy*, also known as *emotional intelligence*. The major insight and strategy of emotional literacy is the ability to notice, rather than ignore, deny, or dismiss, feelings and emotions as they arise, so that you can manage them appropriately. So, for example, you might feel the beginnings of irritation because someone is doing something you dislike. Instead of ignoring these feelings and perhaps letting them build up into an anger that cannot be contained, you notice the actual sensations and feelings of the irritation. It is then, in being aware of them, that you can manage them and deal with both yourself and others more positively.[7] There are great benefits to this reflective and healing meditation. I have known people who use it to self-heal terrible childhood abuse. They have the courage to quietly feel their depth of emotion and pain, and slowly and carefully over time bring it all into their awareness for acceptance and integration. Usually, this depth of healing is also accompanied by the support of an experienced spiritual companion or therapist.

Less dramatically, this form of daily self-awareness is also a very effective way of looking after your physical health. Sitting quietly, pausing, and watching with a kind attitude, you can notice how your body feels and catch early symptoms of a possible illness, which is the foundation of front-end health care and preventative medicine.

EXERCISE
SELF-HEALING MEDITATION

Take yourself into a state of embodied calm, connection, and kind watchfulness using the strategies of the Inner Smile and natural meditation described above.

Or take advantage of a moment when you find yourself in that ambience. Perhaps you can do it commuting to work on the train or bus. Perhaps lying in bed first thing in the morning or before you go to sleep. Or slowly walking. Whatever and whenever works for you.

Stay there as long as you like, resting and watching.

If for any reason you start to feel agitated or impatient or uncomfortable, experiment with noticing the rise and fall of your breath.

Guide yourself to maintain your kind and watchful attitude.

Carefully scan your body to notice any sensations of tension or discomfort. If there are any, stay present to them, just observing the sensation, accepting it, breathing. Be very patient.

Any irritable sensations or thoughts are normal. Greet them as old friends. Notice how they feel. Just watch.

Usually, irritability will fade away as you stay watchful, embodied, and connected.

Allow a challenging part of your life to come into your thoughts. Notice the sensations that accompany it. Be caring and compassionate toward your feelings and thoughts.

If any feelings or thoughts seem to be overwhelming, push them away, distance them. You can allow them to come back when you are ready.

Stay relaxed and sunk into your abdomen. Soft eyes. Open heart. Kind mind.

As you accept everything about yourself, sooner or later distress will evaporate. The key is to be patient and accepting.

Before you end this exercise, always come home to being embodied, connected, and kindly watchful.

THE PARADOXICAL OPPORTUNITY OF CRISIS AND ILLNESS

One of the great benefits of a spiritual outlook is that we can look with some philosophical dispassion at our own illnesses and disasters, manage them, and be grateful for the opportunity to learn. It is wonderful and redemptive how the human spirit can wake up in times of discomfort, pain, and challenge. Our compassion and witnessing consciousness can emerge and grow in the most uncomfortable of situations.

Paradoxically, then, irritability, dissatisfaction, and even pain can be helpful to you, because they tickle to the surface your instinct to grow your heart and awareness. In times of illness, failed relationships, financial downturns, and career failures, where else is your spirit to go? The actual physical circumstances cannot be controlled, but your consciousness and your heart are nevertheless free to break through into new realizations. You heart can open. Your mind can awaken.

EXERCISE
GRATITUDE AND AWAKENING

Take a few minutes to contemplate.

Sink into yourself and guide your attitude into that of the Inner Smile, focusing with kindness and care on your own body and feelings.

Become aware of the earth, natural world, sun, and cosmos—of spirit, the wonder and energy.

Allow yourself to feel its hum and beneficence.

Bring into your awareness something in your life that is causing you distress.

Keep it at a mental distance and look kindly at your distress.

Recognize that in this moment you have the discipline and strength to be detached from the situation and your distress.

Congratulate yourself on being able to be detached and wise.

Notice that your distress is very small compared with the vast mystery of creation.

Notice that your distress has helped to wake you up and bring you to this point of watchfulness and connection.

If it feels appropriate and authentic, give thanks for the situation that has caused you distress. Give thanks for its education and its ability to awaken you.

Then relax back into just feeling your connection.

So it is that people often describe the hidden blessing of illness—and waking up to a new kind of awareness—within a spiritual context. In a poignant and dramatic form, we can see it in fatal illnesses, when an individual may say, "My body may be dying, but I am healed. I am changed and awake." In his moving book *Healing Into Life and Death*, Stephen Levine, a pioneer in the field of understanding the spiritual growth that can happen during sickness, describes the final months of a man, Bill, dying from terminal illness. Bill has tried all forms of medical intervention, including all the different holistic and complementary approaches, but none of them has worked. Finally, Bill realizes that he needs to accept his own death and discovers a deep new level of self-acceptance and self-compassion, which he calls his real healing. In an open letter shortly before his death, Bill wrote,

> And so my healing has occurred. Soon my body will drop away from me like a healing cocoon and my spirit will fly like a butterfly—beautiful and perfect. I don't claim to know exactly where it is that I am going, but my heart tells me that it is filled with light and love. An open heart is a much greater blessing than death is a tragedy. Let us all take comfort in this knowledge.[8]

This is the true nobility of the human spirit, our ability to wake up in the midst of fear and pain. I am particularly touched by his insight that "an open heart is a much greater blessing than death is a tragedy."

I do not wish these sad situations on anyone, but they often contain this spiritual growth, which a group of Canadian social workers dubbed "post-traumatic development," because they kept seeing people go through terrible events and circumstances, yet nevertheless be redeemed by deep and positive insights and change.[9]

This opportunity for spiritual growth is the paradoxical blessing of tough times. As Margaret Newman, a professor of nursing, wrote in her book *Health as Expanding Consciousness*, we human beings are always doing wellness and illness.[10] It is normal life for us to be always moving between health and sickness. The real issue, she suggests, is not whether we are ill or well. The real issue, whatever our state of health, is how our compassion and consciousness are developing. That, she also suggests, is the true purpose of nursing: to nurture the soul's growth.

EMPTYING AND UNKNOWING

Finally, before I end this chapter, I want to wave a flag for two great allies of reflection and self-management: emptying and unknowing. This is the ability simply to let go of all our usual drives to be busy and engaged and release the need to understand what is going on. It allows a state of being blank. I am not suggesting this is a good state to be in permanently, but it is definitely an important skill to hold in our spiritual toolbox and to use when necessary—which, for those of us caught up in the busyness of modern life, is often.

One of the greatest struggles of contemporary life is that many of us are exposed relentlessly to never-ending information, stimulation, and choices. Harnessed to this is our natural human disposition toward impatience when confronted with stuff we do not like, and the compulsion of our minds for easy and quick answers. Most of us are uncomfortable with waiting or not understanding what is happening.

But, from a spiritual perspective, there is another framework and context. The reality is that we do not know the answers to any of the Big Questions. We do not know how the universe was created. We do not know the ultimate destiny and meaning of creation. We do not even really know what will happen tomorrow.

But we do love to know all the endless little things. The internal chatter and babble is unremitting. It is our job to know and to have an opinion. We chit and chat with the same engagement and seriousness as apes have when they pick and lick fleas off each other.

But notice what happens when you sink into a state of embodied and connected goodwill. There you are bobbing in your state of connection, soaking in the benevolent field, benevolently watching the world. You do not need to know and understand what is happening.

One of the finest things in the world is to be able to shrug and just say, "I don't know—and that's fine."

In mystic Christianity this is described as *emptying*. I remember one Christian friend looking at all the courses available on a program I was directing. "So much noise," she said, "so much stuff. Shouldn't people be emptying instead of filling?"

Her sentiment echoed *The Cloud of Unknowing*, the fourteenth-century Christian manual in which an anonymous mystic gives advice to monks new to the spiritual path. The major counsel is clear. Just empty yourself and, in a mood of humility and gratitude, surrender to the connection. At one point, the Christian mystic writes, "Be willing to be blind, and give up all longing to know the why and how, for knowing will be more of a hindrance than a help."[11]

Exercise
OASES OF NOURISHMENT

As part of your reflection and self-management, you may consider the oases of nourishment that can come from moments of emptiness and unknowing.

Take a few minutes' quiet time for yourself.

With compassion and good humor, recognize that your general busyness will be experienced in physical sensations of tension.

Recognize, too, that your brain and mind will also be in a state of arousal, playing with all the usual thoughts and quandaries.

So allow yourself a big sigh.

Take a deep, long breath and simultaneously raise your shoulders.

Hold your breath and hold your shoulders up for a few seconds.

Then release your breath and drop your shoulders.

Allow your chest and stomach to relax.

Have a warm and compassionate attitude toward yourself.

Recognize the infinite mystery and wonder of creation and the cosmos.

Say to yourself something like, "I do not understand the great mystery of life.

"I am content to understand nothing and be in a state of unknowing.

"I am content and empty."

As thoughts and feelings arise, greet them as welcome guests or as clouds passing in the sky. As best you can, let them go. Repeat the sentiment:

"I do not understand the great mystery of life.

"I am content to understand nothing and be in a state of unknowing.

"I am content and empty."

CHAPTER 4

THE CHALLENGES OF SPIRITUAL GROWTH

✳

In the previous chapter I mentioned a woman who complained that I was not cheering her up. Understandably, because of her melancholia, she wanted me just to focus on the wonder and encouragement of spirituality. But, realistically, it would be a form of denial, and almost irresponsible, to ignore the challenges and difficulties that some people do indeed face on the spiritual path. Discussing these challenges is not just about how being forewarned is to be forearmed. It is to do with having a complete picture of the spiritual landscape and nurturing what might be naive idealism into something wiser.

In this chapter, therefore, we are going to look with compassion and clarity at the possible hazards we face on the spiritual path. This, I warn you, is going to take us into some deep and uncomfortable territory. My hope is that, by meeting these challenges with honesty and care, far from depressing you, this whole subject will deepen your ability to love, evoke your wisdom, and also inspire you as you appreciate more fully how people transform, emerge like phoenixes from the ashes of their crises, and conduct their heroic spiritual journeys.

At the same time, through this process of addressing the shadow side of spirituality and having an honest look at the psychological realities, we will also be able to understand and disarm those more unpleasant religious ideas, such as human unworthiness and original sin.

YOUR HEROIC JOURNEY

We do need to be careful, because we know only too well that spirituality is sometimes not all light and love. I could pretend, like a friendly spiritual salesperson promising easy happiness, that your journey toward being spiritually connected, compassionate, and conscious will be fluffy and easy. But we are creatures of emotion, instinct, flesh, and blood—and we therefore may also behave in ways that cause suffering to ourselves and to others. Is there anyone who is free of the human condition?

We all carry our psychological baggage. Even when connected to the wonder and energy of creation, we can still resist change. We can be moved by the beauty of the night sky, gasp at the magic of creation, soak in the energy of benevolence—and the next moment we behave like irritable twits.

There may be moments of great love and grace, when spiritual growth comes easily, but in general most of us will struggle with our human condition—our resistance, sabotaging, and desires—and there is no spiritual tradition of any wisdom that pretends otherwise. That said, I still wish there were a magic wand that could touch us all with therapeutic stardust.

Long before the insights of modern psychology, it was well understood that the spiritual path could be difficult. Hercules, for example, was a metaphor for everyman on the spiritual path: all of the terrible labors he faced are symbolic of the challenges of spiritual transformation. He had to slay the many-headed Hydra, the heads representing the varied and cunning ways we may all resist becoming more compassionate. He had to clean out the Augean stables, where our internal beasts deposit their manure. And he had to capture the

Cretan bull, representing the bloody-minded willfulness of our pure egoism.

Look, too, at the wonderful Indian paintings of serene meditators sitting cross-legged in bliss. Why do terrible beasts, ghouls, and licking flames so often surround these meditators? These paintings depict the human predicament. At the center is the meditator, reflective and calmly connecting with spirit. Around the meditator are all the daemons, representing our psychological problems.

The lotus flower, floating serenely and beautifully on a still pond, is an Eastern symbol for awakened human spirituality. But look closely at this symbol. The stalk and roots of this beauty pass down through the water, symbolic of human emotion and illusion, into the mud of our earthiness.

In fact, the problems associated with belief and spirituality are so obvious that many good thinkers—atheistic, Marxist, Freudian, puritan, scientific, philosophical—have judged the whole project of spiritual development to be absurd and infantile.

Paradoxically, the world religions, in one way or another, also often take a dim and judgmental view of being human, which you may recall is why they say it is difficult for us to have direct spiritual experiences. In the religions of the Book—Judaism, Christianity, and Islam—God is perfect and we humans are not. We were in the Garden of Eden, but could not resist the serpent, ate the forbidden apple, and the outcome is that we are wicked and sinful.

The major Eastern religions such as Hinduism, Buddhism, Sikhism, and Taoism describe the same condition but from another angle. In their worldviews we are in a long process of reincarnation, a succession of many lives, which we begin as lowly animals, overwhelmed by our instincts. We then slowly, life by life, caste by caste, elevate ourselves through good works and diligent spiritual practice, but we are easily sucked back by our animalistic origins and karma.

East or West, this understanding of human nature is pretty dismal. Put bluntly, we are either sinners or willfully ignorant beasts. I can

121

hear Brian's mother in *Monty Python's Life of Brian*, with her squawk-ing voice: "Humanity is a very naughty species."

But, all of that acknowledged, we do, too, show remarkable love, compassion, and generosity. Also, when we commit to the spiritual path, we do transform and grow. Little wonder, then, that Joseph Campbell, one of the world's finest scholars of spiritual mythology, called the process of human growth "the hero's journey."

One of the oldest known prayers in the world is from the Hindu Brhadaranyaka Upanishad and passionately describes the journey:

> O Lord, lead me from the false, deluding, earthly joys and pleasures to the Eternal Truth of Bliss of the Divine within. *Lead me from igno-rance to wisdom.*
>
> O Lord, lead me from the darkness of ignorance binding me to this perishable body into the Eternal Light of the Soul Divine within. *Lead me from darkness to light.*
>
> O Lord, lead me from death to the Eternal Life, Divine, of oneness with you, within and all around for ever, and make me immortal. *Lead me from death to immortality.*

To put these sentiments in less devotional language, in our trans-formational process we are seeking to move from:

ignorance	→	wisdom
fear	→	love
confusion	→	illumination
lost	→	enlightened
neurosis	→	harmony
unconscious	→	conscious
disconnected	→	connected
self-centered	→	holistic
asleep	→	awake
selfish	→	generous

imprisoned	→	liberated
hate	→	compassion
resentment	→	forgiveness

This is a challenging journey and it is heroic, but there is a deep optimism and vitality in spirituality that comes from our experience of the sheer brilliance of creation—of which we are always a part. Just as it is natural for water to follow gravity down to the ocean or for a tree to reach up toward sunlight, so it is natural for us to develop and transform into beings of compassion and consciousness.

THE SPIRITUAL ILLNESSES

A very beautiful aspect of compassion and consciousness is the practice of meticulous love. Not a sentimental or intrusive emotion, but an engaged and attentive interest that seeks to support and help. If ever you have washed someone's cut, graze, or wound, you will know the kind of love that is needed. Your presence is reassuring. At the same time you must give careful attention to the wound, looking for what needs to be cleaned and the depth of the wound. And, equally important, you know when to step back and get out of the way, supporting your companion's freedom and independence.

The human condition, too, requires careful attention and understanding, and, across many different cultures, those men and women who are specialists in spiritual connection—priests, priestesses, shamans—are also the same people who give pastoral and medical care.

Medicine and hospitals arose out of spiritual communities. In tribal peoples, the medicine woman or medicine man is also the local priest. The phrase *medicine man* literally means "priest." Connecting with the wonder and energy of creation goes hand in hand with caring for one another.

This type of pastoral care is something you too can give. One of the democratic aspects of the new spirituality is that spiritual health care, care for the soul, is no longer a specialist role, but something that belongs to all of us. But, to care for our souls and for each other, we need to be well informed. Managing our health, for example, we all understand the need for exercise, right diet, and a supportive lifestyle. We also know the basic symptoms of common illnesses, and most of us have a cabinet somewhere filled with assorted medicines.

Similarly, we need also to be aware of and understand the common illnesses of spirituality. Here are some of the basic issues:

- Why do people resist change even when they know what is good for them?

- Why do people believe irrational stuff, instead of being comfortable with unknowing?

- Why do people become evangelical about their beliefs and try to force them on others?

- Why can't people have a rational discussion about their beliefs instead of becoming defensive and aggressive?

- Why do people commit suicide or kill others for their beliefs?

- Why do people on the spiritual path experience dark nights of the soul similar to clinical depression?

- Why do people on the spiritual path experience spiritual emergencies similar to nervous breakdowns and psychosis?

These are dramatic issues, and I am not suggesting that everyone on the spiritual path will experience them, but, even so, you cannot deny that they are common problems and very relevant to anyone seriously interested in spirituality. This is obviously a sensitive area, partly because some people want to romanticize the spiritual path and ignore its challenges, and partly because people caught up in these spiritual illnesses usually believe themselves to be healthy.

Furthermore, many people endure poignant emotional and psychological challenges, which we can clearly see in recent National Health Service statistics. In England alone in 2009, there were thirty-nine million prescriptions for antidepressants and sixty million for hypertension and heart failure; there were another eight million prescriptions for psychoses and related disorders. You probably know someone who has endured depression, anxiety, nervous exhaustion, or mental confusion.

Spirituality is not separate from these human psychological realities and it never has been; and so, by the end of this chapter, I want you to have some better and practical understanding of these issues. In the modern world we can all be of service in this area.

AN INTENSE AWAKENING

To illustrate these issues in action, I want to look at a couple of stories, which are quite dramatic and unusual. I am not suggesting that these stories are the norm or that people on the spiritual path are bound to experience something like them, but they help to paint a full picture, and from them we can gain useful insights that will support our own ability to help and care.

This first story is of a young man who experienced an intense and sudden crisis in which his spiritual awakening happened too fast and severely disoriented him. He came out of it all, however, healthy, transformed, and enjoying life.

Neil, in his late twenties, was on a weeklong residential course I led on spiritual practice for people interested in a holistic and multi-faith approach. He was a science teacher in a private boarding school, sporty, kind, and intelligent, but always tense and uncomfortable if he was asked to share about his personal feelings. Self-awareness was completely new to him, and he had never previously thought about either self-management or self-healing.

In fact, he was sitting on an emotional powder keg because, as we found out later, although he had strong creative instincts, he had been brought up in a military family to behave like a brave little soldier. His father, grandfather, and great-grandfather had all been officers. As a child, when upset, he had received no affection, but was brought up to be stoic. He had artistic tendencies but was guided away from them into studying science. He had, however, managed to rebel against the family tradition of a military career and had trained as a science teacher. He had had a few relationships, but none of them had been successful. His sex life had been clumsy and unsatisfying. He had never fully lost his temper, only ever simmered. He had never fully expressed himself or his creative energy.

You can see, then, that he was emotionally very armored and sitting on top of a pressure cooker of repressed feelings and creative energy.

He had been initially attracted to spirituality through books that linked science with meditation and Eastern mysticism, such as *The Tao of Physics* and *The Dancing Wu Li Masters*. Following on from these books, he took up meditation and yoga, which he was really enjoying. Often in meditation he felt that he was communing with God and experiencing the bliss fields of cosmic consciousness. He took this very seriously and was very intense when he communicated about it.

In my course, he was now meeting something quite new for him because I was leading a process that integrated emotional and psychological understanding into spiritual awareness. This meant that people were not discussing their spirituality in a detached and academic way but were being very open and transparent about their challenges, their personal histories, emotional wounds, and experiences. At the same time, he was also now spending several hours a day in meditation in the college's chapel and enjoying his deepening connection.

With the wisdom of hindsight it is possible to see how his crisis arose. He was sitting on a cauldron of repressed emotions. He was connecting intensely through his meditation with the energy and hum of the universe. He was in a group dynamic that was asking him to look at his emotional history and his feelings. He was opening up too fast.

Indeed, finally it all did become too much for him and he went into what is sometimes called a spiritual emergency, a crisis.

In an afternoon session, people in the group were sharing about their family histories and how they affected their ability to open up to spirit. One participant had just spoken about how she had been bullied by her family, and she had started to weep, the rest of the group responding with warmth and care.

At this point, Neil could no longer hold back his repressed emotions. He felt a rush of almost uncontrollable energy and emotion rolling through his body. He tried to control it and tensed up, but as he tensed, he began to tremble. His experience of unmanageable energy became even more intense, and he lost mental control. He had never experienced anything like this before, and his mind was shaken into a state of incomprehension. Seeking to interpret what was happening to him, his mind grasped at any kind of story that would make sense of this engulfing experience.

Suddenly, tense and shaking, he stood up and in a booming voice announced to the group that he was Moses and was here to lead us all into a new age. Most of the group were frightened by his behavior, and he could see their anxious reaction. He was a good-hearted man and instinctively did not want to frighten them, and he was now thrown into further confusion.

I went to him and he collapsed into my embrace and began to weep. For the next forty-eight hours a team of careful helpers looked after him until he was calm and able to self-manage. Obviously he was shaken and he was also embarrassed, but this was the beginning of his true awakening. He could emerge from his old persona and social identity and develop himself authentically. He now looks back and sees his "emergency" as, in fact, a healthy process of emergence.

(In appendix B I give some resources for people or carers experiencing this type of spiritual awakening.)

Before going on to our second story, I just want to point out that his crisis might seem extreme from one perspective, but in a spiritual context it is not so unusual. In many traditions it is understood that we might be filled with divine energy and even taken over by it, causing us to shake and feel overwhelmed. Speaking in tongues and voices is another phenomenon common to intense religious experiences, when people lose a sense of who they are and create a temporary new persona.

MOTHER TERESA'S DEPRESSION

Our second story is different and the opposite of overexcitation. It is about depression and the ongoing melancholia endured by Mother Teresa of Calcutta.

Born in Albania in 1910, Mother Teresa had an early calling to become a nun. As a young woman, she had deep and enduring experiences of direct connection with God. Then, filled with compassion and a deep desire to live a life of service, she heard God's voice talking to her, calling her to serve the sickest, the destitute, and the dying. With no resources other than what she gained from begging, she began her ministry in the worst slums of Calcutta. She created a space where people could be cared for and die in dignity. From nothing she built an international organization for the dispossessed, and in 1979 she received the Nobel Peace Prize for her work.

Her whole life was dedicated to the relief of suffering, and she never faltered in this work of bringing comfort, but for decades she privately endured a profound melancholy and depression. This all became public in 2007 when *Come Be My Light—The Private Writings of the "Saint of Calcutta"* was published.

Although her working life as a nun had begun with a series of peak experiences in which she experienced direct communion with

God, those peaks never happened again. She still felt an ongoing divine presence in the background of her life, but she felt bereft of the ecstatic connection that she had previously experienced and was now in an ongoing state of depression.

Her internal language for self-understanding, however, was not that of modern psychology, but that of Roman Catholicism. Not aware, therefore, that she was caught in one of the tragic human states that so many endure, depression, she interpreted her condition as a form of abandonment and punishment. At one point in the 1950s she wrote:

> Lord, my God, who am I that You should forsake me? The child of your love—and now become as the most hated one—the one You have thrown away as unwanted—unloved. I call, I cling, I want—and there is no One to answer—no One on Whom I can cling—no, No One. Alone. . . . I am told God loves me—and yet the reality of darkness and coldness and emptiness is so great that nothing touches my soul.

"If I ever become a saint I will surely be one of 'darkness,'" she wrote later, in 1959. "I will continually be absent from heaven—to light the light of those in darkness on earth."[1]

Caught in the terrible feelings of depression, her mind created this tragic drama of worthlessness.

These two stories of Neil and Mother Teresa are of course dramatic, and most of us will never experience that kind of extremity. Nevertheless, within each of us are tendencies toward those states, so they help to illustrate what any of us might have to face on a lesser scale.

There are two dynamics here that we need to understand more fully and that have a profound influence on spiritual development. The first is to do with the mental mechanism that controlled how Neil and Mother Teresa interpreted their experience. You may not have thought that you were Moses or that God was punishing you, but you will have experienced times when your mind, almost beyond your control, has invented stories that were untrue. For instance, someone may have promised to contact you, but then did not. Your mind probably spun around a bit, fabricating tales to explain the event.

The second relevant dynamic is the polarity in life and spiritual development between the extremes, at worst, of deep depression on the one side and manic hyperactivity on the other. You, I hope, have not experienced such polarities, but will, just as part of ordinary human life, be aware of the normal mood swings between sad and happy, melancholic and excited. They are not unusual.

THE RELENTLESS ENGINE OF THE MONKEY MIND

So let us look at the first of the great problems that can get in the way of our spirituality: our minds. They are wonderful. They can reflect, analyze, contemplate, assess, and consider. But they are also relentless factories of imagination and story—endless babble and a source of suffering.

This dynamic is described by the term *monkey mind*, a classical Chinese term first used over two thousand years ago, which describes how the human brain keeps on chattering, giving a commentary, and telling itself stories, often with a dynamism that is disturbed, illogical, and compulsive.[2] In Buddhist and Taoist teachings the monkey mind is often described as the great enemy of meditation, but it does far worse things than just sabotage meditation.

Our monkey minds cannot tolerate the anxiety and arousal triggered by ambiguity and unknowing. How do you feel when you are in the middle of watching a television show and someone switches channels? How do you feel when a loved one is traveling far from home and has promised to contact you the moment he or she arrives—and you hear nothing? How do you feel when waiting to hear if you have succeeded in getting a job or making a team or winning a competition?

The Challenges of Spiritual Growth

All these situations of unknowing trigger arousal, anxiety, tension, and even anger. We experience primal frustration when we do not know how a story ends. Our monkey mind makes up imaginary stories to fill in the gaps. This, in fact, is the major purpose of the monkey mind: to create narratives that interpret and explain anything that our nervous system is experiencing. Its job is to create a narrative that makes sense of the current experience and then leads to an action that ensures survival.

It is this ability to create and interpret a narrative that partly enabled the evolution and survival of our species. Our brains evolved to hold, for example, a timeline and mental pictures of the timing and paths of animal migrations, the likely behavior of our companions in various circumstances, the passage of the seasons, the growth cycles of plants. These are narratives that we naked apes must be able to follow and to interpret in order to survive.

In us as a species, our nervous systems, brains, and minds have evolved so that we can create, follow, and interpret these narratives. Our brains have the ability to conjecture and to make imaginative jumps. Dark clouds indicate rain, so we deduce that animals will go to the river that was previously dry and we will be able to hunt them and feed. But there is only a dark cloud. The human brain is then creating the story, filling in the gaps.

Without such a narrative, we are left in the nightmare world of not knowing how we shall survive, not knowing what may happen next. If we do not know what will happen next, if we do not have a satisfactory story, we experience arousal.

Our minds jump to these conclusions relentlessly and automatically. It is a compulsive and necessary unconscious behavior that we all endure. If we do not have a satisfactory conclusion or interpretation, our minds, faced with a state of nothingness, manufacture interpretations and stories to relieve the arousal and fill in the unbearable gaps.

131

This phenomenon is known in neuroscience as confabulation. The psychiatrist and literary scholar Iain McGilchrist graphically described confabulation as "where the brain, not being able to recall something, rather than admit to a gap in its understanding, makes up something plausible, that appears consistent, to fill it. . . . The left hemisphere [of the brain] is the equivalent of the sort of person who, when asked for directions, prefers to make something up rather than admit to not knowing."[3]

The greatest irony of all this mind chatter is that we believe what our minds make up. The man who invents the directions believes, in that moment, that what he is saying is real and true. Moreover, once your monkey mind has fabricated a particular story, it then has a tendency to cling to it, resisting new or contradictory information, sometimes for years. When someone ignored you several years ago, for example, you may have fabricated a story of disrespect, which stays with you, despite the fact that the person was simply distracted or caught up in his or her own overwhelming problems.

This storytelling compulsion is also at the heart of psychological projection, how we project stories onto other people. We might meet someone who reminds us of our father, and our mind then projects onto this person that he will behave in the same way as our father. We have projected a narrative onto this innocent screen. We might also meet someone, for example, who looks like the perfect object of our desire, and off our mind gallops, projecting high romance or tragic rejection onto this person, before even a word has been exchanged.

In psychotherapy this monkey-mind compulsion to confabulate and make up stories is also known as *rationalization*. This is when people invent an apparently reasonable story to explain and justify irrational feelings and behavior. In the words of the American Psychiatric Association's *Diagnostic and Statistical Manual of Mental Disorders*, the authoritative psychiatric diagnostic manual in the English-speaking world, rationalization occurs "when the individual deals with emotional conflict or internal or external stressors by concealing the true motivations for his or her own thoughts, actions, or feelings through the elaboration of reassuring or self-serving but incorrect explanations."[4]

This "elaboration of reassuring or self-serving but incorrect explanations," is something we all do. Unable to face a threatening reality, we make up little stories. This happens, for example, all the time when we fail to deliver a promise to someone on time and then meet the person: "Didn't you receive it?" "I was just about to send it." "I did send it." "It must be lost." The unconscious process for fixing an uncomfortable situation is so fast that we often do not know what we are saying until we hear it coming out of our own mouths.

THE NORMALITY OF "VOICES"

If we immediately apply this knowledge to the experiences of Neil and Mother Teresa, we can see how their minds, desperate to interpret their experiences, created coherent stories that at the time made sense of what was happening to them. Most "delusions" make sense once we look through them into the underlying experience stimulating their fabrication.

With Neil we can see the dam of emotion bursting, but we also know he was in the process of opening up too fast to the field of spiritual energy. He was caught in a double wave of intensity that overwhelmed his nervous system and his ability to remain stable. His monkey mind confabulated that he was Moses leading us into a new age. In that moment, inside that experience, there was a real logic to that interpretation.

In Mother Teresa's case, she was in a state of ongoing melancholia following the loss of her early intense spiritual experiences and, in the language of the prayers and sentiments of her faith, her interpretation too is perfectly consistent.

Inside their experience, their interpretations make sense, even though of course their interpretations are not literally true. Neil was not Moses. Nor was Teresa being punished. But their stories were accurate metaphors of their internal experience.

We need also to appreciate that in crises of this kind, the delusion will be amplified by the psychological dynamics of, for example, childhood distress or abuse. We can see clearly how Neil's emotionally frigid childhood fed into the intensity of his awakening. It is possible too that Mother Teresa's interpretation was colored by her strict family upbringing. Also, in the view of some spiritual psychologists, these interpretations may be strongly influenced by past lives, archetypes, and genetic and ancestral memories.[5]

Sometimes these confabulations and stories can even be heard inside people's heads as separate voices, seemingly disassociated, as if from outside. Nowadays there is usually a nervous knee-jerk reaction when we hear that someone "hears voices," but as Daniel Smith, a journalist who researched this subject because of his father's diagnosis as a psychotic, points out, hearing voices used to be considered a normal occurrence that occasionally happened to everybody. The real issue is whether the voices are helpful or destructive.[6]

Certainly, if we understand that monkey mind chatter is an unavoidable and unconscious compulsive neural behavior seeking to relieve anxiety and arousal, then the weirdest thoughts and voices can be understood as just part of the normal ecology of our minds.

THE BUNGEE CORDS OF RESISTANCE

But the effect of our monkey minds cannot be fully understood unless we also understand the dynamics of attachment and resistance to change.

We all tend to hang on to our stuff. When we know we ought to change, we do not. Even when we know that there is a magic and beauty to creation, and that our life's essential purpose is to become more loving and conscious, we may remain the same, sometimes like limpets.

I do not write about this as a detached observer or educator. I write as someone who also wrestles with my resistance and my self-sabotage. Sometimes I have even felt some despair about this. If the cosmos is so filled with wonder and energy, why is it that we do not *easily* develop into compassionate beings? If the universe is so benevolent, why is change so hard? Decades ago I committed my life to spiritual development and, day by day, I have done my spiritual practice—connection, reflection, and service. I am seriously engaged. Anyone who knows me, including my family and my critics, will say that I do my best to walk my talk. Yet I am still regularly sucked back into old behaviors, feelings, and patterns of thought.

And I expect some readers might now want to send me a sympathetic message. It's all right, William. You're *just human*. Thank you, I am grateful for that compassionate empathy, but I still want to look at why it is that we resist the flow and benevolence of the cosmos and cling to our old negative stuff.

Before exploring the metaphysical and psychological causes of this resistance, let me share a few stories to illustrate the issue. In particular we are looking at how people can have a sense of spiritual connection, awaken, commit to personal change, but then slip back into old behaviors.

When I lived in Morocco, for example, two friends—minor playboy types—participated in the *hajj*, the largest annual pilgrimage in the world, when Muslims travel to Mecca and take part in a series of rituals to purify and spiritually awaken. All Muslims are called to do this pilgrimage at least once in their lives, and it is considered an immense life transition.

These two friends returned from their pilgrimage visibly moved by the experience. They were calmer and kinder. They had committed to spiritual change. Their old habits of drinking, shifty business deals, and womanizing stopped. They could now look me directly in the eye. Their shifts were authentic. But over twelve months they slowly slipped back into their old ways. Twenty-five years of playboy behavior were not transformed by a single pilgrimage, no matter how powerful the spiritual experience.

I know a woman, too, who, as the result of a motoring accident, was trapped in a car for five hours. Her body's defense mechanisms kicked in, and she went into an altered state of consciousness in which she experienced no pain and no fear and was filled with feelings and thoughts of love. She spent those five hours soaking in those good feelings and a (deep connection with life's wonder.) All the way through her rescue and then convalescence, she maintained her composure and her inspired mood. In her own words, she felt blessed by the whole event. But then, over several months, she sank back into her previous attitude of cynicism.

This woman and the two pilgrims were profoundly moved by their experiences, but the elastic of their transformation would stretch only so far before pulling back to its original state.

This is not unusual. Everyone, for example, experiences it with New Year resolutions. You will, I am sure, be familiar with having made a resolution to change something and do something new. Get more exercise. Be kinder. Eat better. Stop smoking. Be less critical and judgmental. We may even succeed for a while, but then we slip back. The bungee cords suck us back.

The power of this suction is tangible, not some light psychological whim. Anyone who has experienced cravings knows how powerful, primal, and painful a force they are. If you ever weaned yourself off tobacco, alcohol, chocolate, or sugar, you will probably have experienced the force of the biological compulsion and cravings.

But it is not just substances that create addiction. We are also addicted to attitudes and activities, which demand to be continued. Most of you have probably experienced clear moments of reflective conscience in which you have decided to stop an abusive or destructive behavior. You will not be rude to that person again. You will be kinder. You make that decision, yet you still do not behave in an improved way. The power of the ingrained habit is too strong.

THE PSYCHOLOGY OF RESISTANCE

At the risk of oversimplification, let me present a brief digest of the three generally accepted psychological theories that explain this attachment and self-sabotaging. Anyone interested in spiritual development needs to be aware of them. Again, forgive me for taking us temporarily away from the inspiration and *joie de vivre* of spirituality, but we cannot grow flowers without digging up the earth. These things are crucial for understanding the human condition and spiritual resistance. The ability to integrate psychology is one of the real blessings of modern spirituality. And through this understanding we can achieve much deeper and sustainable growth and well-being and avoid many of the mistakes of previous generations. It will make you so much stronger.

Conditioning

First, there is the theory from the school of *behavioral psychology*, which suggests that, from birth, we are *conditioned*, through rewards and punishments, into habits of behavior. You will be familiar with this approach in the idea of Pavlov's dog, which was conditioned to associate the sound of a bell with food, so that it salivated at the sound of the bell, even when there was no food.

In the same way, our own attitudes are conditioned and embedded in our nervous systems, and unless these behaviors and habits meet an equally strong force of new conditioning, they will resist change. Simply wanting to change is not powerful enough to undo the original conditioning.

So, for example, you may have gotten into the habit of overeating or being defensive when criticized or indulging in inappropriate humor when you were a child, and that behavior has become ingrained and embedded in your nervous system over decades. A simple decision such as a New Year's resolution is not going to easily transform such a deep neural groove.

Chapter 4

Repression

The *psychoanalytic* school of psychology, which originated in the research of Sigmund Freud, then suggests that this conditioning is reinforced by the dynamics of *repression*. Complex and highly sensitive, our nervous systems are unable to manage and respond to all the stimuli we receive. In particular, as children we cannot respond to all the threats and unkindness that happen around us and to us. If we were to respond, we would put ourselves at risk, so we swallow our arousal. These childhood responses are repressed and buried as unconscious but charged memories. These ancient traumas and suppressed reactions then rumble in the background of our lives, influencing our thoughts, emotions, and feelings.

So we may feel and behave in certain ways, but we do not understand the unconscious forces that are motivating us.

Homeostasis

There is then a third theory, which belongs more to *neuroscience*. This theory proposes that the most vital function of the brain and nervous system is *homeostasis*, the maintenance of balance and the status quo. To put it another way, our nervous systems and brains will do whatever is necessary to bring our bodies back to the states to which we are accustomed.

A simple example of this is how we sweat if we become too hot. The perspiration is simply a mechanism for reducing temperature and restoring us to our default temperature. Our nervous systems, therefore, are built to reject automatically any new behavior and attitude, simply because they are new—and always seek to return to our habitual and engrained defaults.

It is important for us to be aware of these important psychological dynamics that are at play in everyone, including ourselves. They are psychological and neural reality, and we cannot ignore them. But we do not need to be controlled by them, and the first step in managing and guiding them effectively is to be aware of them. Again, this is where an attitude of detached compassion toward ourselves, of good-humored watchfulness, the Inner Smile, is so useful. This good-humored self-watchfulness not only allows us to monitor and manage our internal dynamics, but also creates a new set of neural grooves that become embedded and ingrained. Just as we may once perhaps have been addicted to food or rudeness or being a victim, now we are in a deep groove of compassionate witnessing and kindness.

EXERCISE

BEING REALISTIC ABOUT THE PSYCHOLOGY OF RESISTANCE

Pause and take yourself into a centered and watchful state.

Bring into your awareness some behavior or attitude that you committed to change, but have not.

With your Inner Smile of kindness toward yourself, look at that behavior or attitude with compassion and understanding.

Recognize how it is fuelled by

- the unconscious psychological and neural dynamics of your conditioning;

- your unconscious and repressed motives; and

- your nervous system's desire to maintain its status quo.

Just look at it all very calmly.

Be patient and understanding, and know that, by being fully present and recognizing the psychological dynamics, changing that behavior will be easier and more graceful.

In these quiet moments of contemplation, looking carefully and honestly at your behavior supports the whole process of reconditioning it into a new state.

RESISTANCE IS A FORCE OF NATURE

I want to suggest that these psychological dynamics of resistance are also entwined with a force that pervades the natural world and helps to explain the raw power and intensity of some of our attachments. This is the force of raw magnetism or gravity, the cosmic power that holds the cosmos together, including ourselves. This universal agency is described very explicitly in the Taoist model of the two cosmic polarities, Yin and Yang. This is also a very useful psychological model.

Yang describes the force of the Big Bang. Creative, emergent, and expansive. Unimaginably powerful and explosive. It brought all creation into existence.

Yin is the equally powerful force that binds things together—magnetism, gravity, containment—without which there would be no actual creation at all, just inchoate expansion. Without this magnetic force there would be no cosmos as we know it, no galaxies, no stars, no earth, no flowers, no animals, no us. If it were not equal in power, there would be no coherent form. The Taoist sage Shao Yong wrote, "Yang cannot exist by itself; it can exist only when it is supported by Yin."[7]

We can see this same theme surfacing too in all spiritual traditions where deity is described both as Father and as Mother, the Father representing the emergent and expansive force of creation, the Mother representing the containing and magnetic force of creation. We can see them, too, in spiritual cosmologies that feature a polarity between Earth and Heaven.

The universe as we know it, then, is a balance or a dance between these two forces, between expansion and containment, between change and stasis. These two cosmic polarities are also inside us. They make up the actual matter of our bodies, and they also work out in our psychology. This indeed is biological reality, as the cells in our bodies are constantly changing, yet we remain a coherent form.

This polarity between change and stasis, between expansion and containment, works out in many of the natural rhythms of life—between action and rest, awake and asleep, birth and death, sowing and harvest, spring and autumn. It also plays out in our own mood swings and how we are continuously strung out between an instinct to grow and emerge and an instinct to remain the same.

There is a huge insight here, which brings the grace of understanding and forgiveness to what appears to be our unreasonable intransigence and addiction to old things. We are programmed, hard-wired, supported by cosmic forces, both to change and to remain the same. It is part of our function, as aspects of this cosmic dance, to stay glued to who we are. We have no choice in this. Just as we have no choice, too, but to change.

This profound yet startlingly obvious concept—that all creation is a balance between expansion and containment—is not just a philosophical or cosmological insight. It also precisely describes one of the great ambiguities and paradoxes of the human condition: we are strung out between growth and resistance.

If you have ever been despondent about your resistance to change, there is huge comfort here. Our resistance does not derive from some innate weakness or sinfulness or bad karma. Our resistance to change and the way that we hang on to old habits derive from a cosmic and natural force that combines with the three psychological dynamics of conditioning, repression, and homeostasis. No wonder we can sometimes find it difficult. But at least, understanding the underlying reasons, we no longer have to feel shame about it. It is just one of the underlying structures of human nature and underlines, it seems to me, the heroic and brilliant way in which we do indeed emerge and grow.

Chapter 4

THE HUMAN PARADOX OF TENSION

YANG ←	→ YIN
EMERGENCE ←	→ GRAVITY
EXPANSION ←	→ CONTAINMENT
CHANGE ←	→ COHERENCE
MOVEMENT ←	→ MAGNETISM
MALE ←	→ FEMALE
FATHER ←	→ MOTHER
ACTIVITY ←	→ STASIS
WE WANT TO CHANGE ←	→ *WE WANT TO STAY THE SAME*

UNDERSTANDING THE HIGHS AND THE LOWS

One way, then, of looking at spiritual psychology and human moods is to see that it is perfectly natural for us to move between these two dynamics of containment and expansion, between moods of depression and elation, because this is the inevitable *felt* and existential result of being caught in this dance between the two cosmic forces. These polarities can also be intensified by our growing spiritual connection and increased sensitivity.

In an everyday way, we all experience these downs and ups in our mood swings, low energy to high energy, unhappy to happy, depressed to elated. Some changes we find easy and others are more difficult. This is normal human experience.

But this normal experience can also go to extremes that are painful and full of suffering. At one end of the spectrum, magnetism and gravity, we find a lack of energy, melancholy, and a sense of depressing containment in which nothing makes sense. At the other end of the spectrum, we find too much energy and manic physical, emotional, and mental activity, with a loss of self-control. Some of these extreme moods may last months or even years. Other times their alternating rhythm may be more staccato.

I need to tread very carefully here, because I do not want to make light of depression or manic behavior, especially when it is accompanied by psychotic delusions, which require expert medical care. Nor do I want to appropriate serious psychological suffering and trivialize it by speculating that it is all a meaningful spiritual process. I do, however, want to relieve these conditions of their stigma and stop seeing them as wild animals in uncharted territory.

From a wider perspective, these illnesses are extremes of what we all experience, albeit in a much milder form. This understanding might therefore, when appropriate and manageable, bring these illnesses into a more self-manageable condition, using compassionate self-reflection and mindfulness.

Certainly, when you become troubled by these painful and disorienting states of mood swings, melancholy and resistance, inspiration and self-sabotage, overexcitement and nervous exhaustion, you will find enduring relief by coming home to the basic strategies of the Inner Smile and compassionate watchfulness. It is here, in being centered and connected, embodied and kind to yourself, philosophically good-humored and observant, that you will find the tools for ongoing self-management.

Again, at the risk of oversimplification, it is possible to map out a general chart of how these forces of containment and expansion might affect your behavior. Awareness of the spectrum is helpful.

Referring to the Yin dynamic of magnetism and coherence, we can suggest the following:

- BALANCED CONTAINMENT: We feel safe, coherent, and stable.

- TOO MUCH CONTAINMENT: We feel flat, sluggish, and lazy; we have no energy for change.

- FAR TOO MUCH CONTAINMENT: We feel melancholic and apathetic.

- EXTREME CONTAINMENT: We sink into depression, inertia, and the dark night of the soul.

Oppositely, when referring to the Yang dynamic of emergence and expansion, we can suggest the following:

- BALANCED EXPANSION: We feel movement, growth, and flow.

- TOO MUCH EXPANSION: We feel scattered, speedy, and irritable.

- FAR TOO MUCH EXPANSION: We feel overstimulated, hyper, and cannot sleep; we feel that we are burning out.

- EXTREME EXPANSION: We feel emotionally and mentally out of control, in a spiritual emergency, manic, in a nervous breakdown.

CONFABULATION AND THE GREAT MYTHS

Now, let's put all of this together and be realistic about what it brings. We have here several powerful ingredients that mix together in this recipe:

- our monkey minds' compulsive storytelling;

- our mood swings, sometimes between depression and mania; and

- our resistance and addictions.

Place all these in a highly sensitive human nervous system that is easily aroused and triggered into anxiety. And then locate this human being in a natural and cosmic environment that is sometimes dangerous and always awesome.

This situation is quite a concoction. Naked apes with cosmic wiring. The human condition. No wonder we need compassion and mindfulness, healing and self-care, courage and discipline. No wonder, too, that we get a species that will on occasion believe absolutely anything—and then cling to this false belief with fury and aggression.

Sometimes when I watch people on the spiritual path, I think we are like newly hatched goslings that latch on to and follow the first moving thing they see. This is not surprising given the psychological dynamics. Our monkey minds' compulsive need for a story that relieves anxiety naturally results in our wanting and falling for the first story that provides some coherence. We fall for it because our vulnerable nervous systems are looking for as fast a dose of comfort as we can get, regardless of the twaddle we have to take in and believe. This is not new: today's quick-fix spiritualities are yesterday's pardons and saints' bones.

Unfortunately, we know only too well that some spiritual teachers, preachers, and gurus may take advantage of this human insecurity and pretend to have, and even be, all the answers. On a grand scale we can see this pretence at knowing everything and having *the* story in all the major religions, which present grand stories—such as God's creation of the universe in seven days—claiming to explain everything: creation, human nature, our destiny and purpose. Many of us latch on to these and may be unable to hear other interpretations of reality. But, as the wise philosopher John Michell, who pioneered a contemporary understanding of sacred geometry and landscape, wryly observed, "The very nature of our existence is a mystery. In the center of human knowledge is a large gap which, for the sake of decency, we cover over with a veil of myths, faiths and theories."[8]

All across human civilization, throughout all time periods, our species has understandably been incapable of tolerating the tension of living inside a universe, inside an existence, that has no story, no narrative that gives meaning to the cosmos in general and human life in particular. All across human culture there are creation myths that seek to explain the inexplicable, to clothe the naked emperor. These creation myths are themselves creations, created to allay anxiety or, at best, as a song of worship to a mysterious universe. Every time the word *God* is used as if the universal mystery were in some way similar to a giant human being, we know that confabulation and projection are at work. As Nobel Prize winner José Saramago wrote through one of his novels' characters, "It's worth considering that the reason so many theories about the origin of the universe have been created since the birth of speech and the word is that all of them, one by one, have failed miserably, with a regularity that augurs rather ill for the one which, with a few variations, is currently in vogue."[9]

This issue is very sensitive and difficult. Religion by religion, to comfort us from the anxiety of unknowing, there are these great myths that explain our world and how we can and should live. In a multi-cultural world, we need to respect this diversity of belief. But, at the same time, we cannot switch off our modern understanding of how the human psyche works and pretend these myths are literal. These grand interpretations are interesting, symbolic, and often beautiful, but they are also dangerous when they become sacred totems and when any questioning of them is considered to be blasphemy.

The real tragedy here is how personal spiritual development is hijacked by a religious ideology and mobilized into a social force that can be used for either good or bad. How positive and hopeful it would be if every priest, priestess, and cleric taught self-reflection, emptying, and unknowing alongside their own sacred scriptures.

This discussion is hugely relevant to us because we have to be careful about what we believe. We might, for instance, believe that it is more important to be knowledgeable about our particular beliefs than to actually practice compassion and awareness. We might judge other people as being ignorant, because they do not understand or practice what we think is essential and we do not see the beauty of their hearts.

EXERCISE
BELIEFS AND UNKNOWING

Take a few minutes to contemplate.

Looking back over your life, recall someone or something you believed in, but later found your belief to be unfounded. Notice how you wanted to believe and to trust.

Have compassion and understanding for that part of your psychology that needs a belief in order to feel safe and stable.

Contemplate the wonder and energy you can sense in nature and the cosmos.

Contemplate the whole mystery of creation and existence, and allow your mind to relax and empty into unknowing.

Consider now whether you are attached to any particular spiritual beliefs. Look at them with detached kindness. Can you let them go?

Relax into unknowing and connection.

MARTYRDOM AND A SENSE OF SELF

It is not just that we latch on to beliefs and stories, but that we also *cling* to them, even unto death. Never underestimate the power with which you are glued to the story that is the narrative of your life. Some people would rather die than relinquish their sense of identity, their story about who they are.

My original doctoral research was around how we create our sense of identity and how, from the moment we are born, we are biologically compelled to respond to our social environment by copying and internalizing the behavior and attitudes of others.

Our characters and our identities, therefore, which we describe as being "psychological," are embedded in us as neural and endocrinologic patterns, which ensure our survival and sense of coherence. We may then defend these patterns of identity right up to and including death. People would often rather die than betray who they think and feel themselves to be. We see this in martyrs and suicide bombers, who sustain their sense of psychological self with no care for physical survival.

Chapter 4

I was shocked into fully understanding this when, as a teenager, I saw photographs of a Vietnamese Buddhist monk, Thích Quang Duc, who emptied a can of petrol over himself and then, sitting cross-legged, set fire to himself and died. He was protesting against the policy of the Vietnamese government, which had banned the display of religious flags, in particular the flags normally flown at the festival of Wesak, the birthday of Gautama Buddha.

Here we have a man, a Buddhist monk steeped in the traditional teachings of meditation, reflection, and detached equanimity, dying this awful death in order to uphold his sense of identity. Such courage! Such paradox! Terrible poignancy.

You and I will never approach that extreme of drastic action, but even so, on a lesser scale, we will tend to defend our stories and identities. Once we have become attached to a particular way of practicing our spirituality, we may well cling to it, and we may well defend it aggressively from curiosity and skepticism, rather than welcoming inquiry and discussion. And, again, we are called, as a solution, to careful reflection.

EXERCISE

LOOKING AT THE STORY OF YOUR LIFE

Take a few minutes to contemplate.

Allow your mind to travel back to your birth and your family. Contemplate your childhood homes and your family. Bring to mind the kind of clothes you wore, your interests, and your friends.

Move forward into your teen years, again picturing yourself, your interests, and your friends.

Move forward decade by decade until the present moment.

Be aware that you can, with compassion and kindness, observe the whole of your story.

You are able to be a witnessing consciousness, just watching everything you have been.

With kindness, contemplate this idea:

I am my story and I am more than my story.

DETACHING YOURSELF FROM YOUR STORY

All the stories we tell ourselves, all the plans we formulate and decisions we make—all of them—may be just the machinations of our attached monkey minds seeking to relieve arousal and anxiety and sustain homeostasis.

This is the tightrope of human consciousness. Which aspect of our thinking and imagining is real and valid and worthwhile? Is everything you believe yourself to be an illusion, conjured up by an anxious nervous system?

The only solution here is benevolent watchfulness and the growth of your loving-witness consciousness. To put it more bluntly, you need to detach yourself from your story. You need the spiritual muscle and the skill, whenever appropriate, to stop taking your story so seriously. Detach yourself from your story and be a benevolent witness to all that you are. Whenever you feel arousal and the need for a narrative that will make you feel better, just back off and watch the process with compassionate equanimity.

We have here again the relevance and usefulness of the four core skills: pause and be mindful; relax, be centered and grounded in your body; observe what is happening in a kind and good-humored way; yield to the feeling of connection.

Chapter 4

In one of my Spiritual Companions courses, my colleagues and I once had a long dialogue with a very intelligent and good-hearted woman who was trapped in unrequited stories and desires about how her life ought to be.

"The most important thing in my life," she said, "is my increasing connection with spirit, but to achieve that I really need to fulfill my life's purpose. I have a real sense that I need to be an independent businesswoman and not an employee. I know that this is my destiny."

"Perhaps," I suggested, "your real destiny is, as you say, to fully connect and also develop your heart and consciousness."

"I am," she agreed, "completely dedicated to that. But, to fulfill that, I need to fulfill myself and get out of my present job. How do you think I can do that?"

"I'm not sure," I replied, "but I wonder if it would be more helpful to focus on your spiritual development."

"That's exactly what I am doing," she reassured me. "I have to get out of that job and into an independent career."

Our conversation carried on in this circular fashion for a while, as I attempted to focus her on developing her heart and consciousness, and she stayed inside her story about a new job and career.

"Perhaps you just want to feel independent," I suggested, trying another tack.

"It seems to me," another student said more directly, "that you want to feel more centered, independent, and confident, and you're blaming your current work situation for not being able to achieve that state. And you've created a story for yourself that the change will only come when you change your circumstances. Why not drop the story and just work on your change right now? Imagine you'll never change your job. Just be present. Here, now. And work on yourself. Drop the story that relies on your future."

For a moment there was a flash of pure rebellion, resistance, and denial. Then she nodded, accepting the logic and truth of what had just been said. Then she sighed.

"Stop obsessing about a new job," she said. "Just be present, center and shift myself. I could do that. And who knows? When I've made the shift, maybe the new career could come anyway." She smiled. "Whoops! That's me inside my story again."

I sympathized, though, with her mental predicament. It is only too easy to get caught up in an inner narrative in which it seems that we can do or be what we want only *after* the right circumstances have been achieved. Over and over again, I have heard students and colleagues say to me that they will be able to do their spiritual practice properly and regularly only once they have a good relationship or a new home, or live in the country or change jobs, and so on. These are all just stories and confabulations justifying the status quo—and we need to be able to see through them. Once again, contemplative reflection serves us.

EXERCISE
WHAT DO WE REALLY NEED?

Take a few minutes to pause.

Allow yourself to relax and sink down into your body.

Let your stomach sink and relax. Soften your attitude, opening your heart, putting a smile in your eyes, and guiding your mind to be kind.

Bring into your awareness some object or goal that you desire. (If you do not desire anything at all, be grateful and move on from this exercise.)

Contemplate what it would *feel* like for you if you achieved your desire.

Spend a while contemplating the idea that what you really want is this *feeling* and not the actual object of your desire.

151

See if you can completely release your desire and focus with kindness on the feeling you want.

Notice that by being fully present, kind, and watchful, you can dispel the desire and reflect on what is really happening within you.

DESIRE IS A SOURCE OF SUFFERING

Our stories can sometimes run obsessively in our heads like rodents in caged wheels, torturing our psyches with images and finales. This perhaps is the most terrible aspect of the monkey mind for those of us who are otherwise healthy and balanced. We become trapped by these unfulfilled stories about ourselves.

Superficially, it may look simply like the desire for a new career or relationship, or a new coat or car; but explore the underlying dynamics. At an unconscious level, you are probably feeling fractionally insecure and vulnerable. This unconscious feeling in turn creates an uncomfortable feeling in your nervous system, which, following the dynamics of homeostasis, creates an interpretive story with a resolution. In this story, your arousal is relieved by your having the new career, relationship, jacket, or car.

All this is happening inside your mind and nervous system, but for real relief, for a real resolution, you try in real life to acquire that job or relationship—and you will be goaded by your arousal and unfulfilled narrative until your desire is consummated. Your nervous system cannot relax back from its state of arousal and anxiety until the story has reached its successful conclusion.

The problem here is twofold. First, your underlying anxiety is never addressed and understood. Second, you become trapped in an obsession that is essentially meaningless, but that feels hugely important and meaningful.

No wonder, then, that Buddha classically taught that desire is the source of all suffering. In a more modern context this is sometimes called "status anxiety."[10] Our monkey minds and nervous systems get caught in a loop of arousal, anxiety, and storytelling to relieve the arousal. Desire is a state of physical and psychological arousal that tortures us until fulfilled. The narrative must have its ending.

Worse still, caught up in the story and the arousal, driven by status anxiety or other emotional needs, we lose our centers, lose our kind watchfulness, and separate from our connection with the wonder and energy of creation.

This obsession with the narrative of our own lives is supremely normal, for we are visceral creatures fully enmeshed in our biology and neurology. We can hardly escape the dynamics that make up our very fabric. Moreover, daydreaming is a great pleasure, and it is also a positive and worthwhile activity to contemplate how our lives *might* be. We do indeed need to plan and make decisions, and these activities are predicated on the creativity of our monkey minds.

But, if we believe that these stories we tell ourselves inside our minds are true and always true, then we are lost. If we believe that the narrative of our identity is the only reality, we are mistaken. At its most paradoxical, I have seen this phenomenon in clergy and members of spiritual communities who have become obsessed with attaining the next level on their spiritual career ladder—becoming bishop, or even archbishop, or in charge of their community's finances.

Again and again, we have to come back to compassionate watchfulness and using the wisdom and insights of reflection and mindfulness. Again and again, too, we have to sink back into our deepest connection with the wonder and energy of creation, with the benevolence of the cosmos, and appreciate that it is in this greater reality that we find our true comfort and life's deepest meaning and joy.

THE ONE-BRAIN-CELL APPROACH

In calm times, it is clear that connection and reflection serve us well, but what are we to do when we experience a storm? The reality of an extreme state or crisis is that, overwhelmed by feelings of depression or frenzy, caught perhaps in a compulsion or desire, our monkey minds may work overtime churning out oppressive chatter, making it difficult, if not impossible, to find our center, our connection, and our compassionate watchfulness.

You may find the solution in using what I call the "one-brain-cell approach." I did not originate the one-brain-cell strategy, but learned it from John, a strong, loving, and attractive man who was one of the leaders of a self-help group of patients who had previously been in psychiatric care and had invited me to come and give a presentation. I turned up with a very cautious attitude, because I was not at all certain that my strategies, based in meditation, were suitable for people emerging from psychiatric care.

John, though, greeted me at the doorway with a beaming smile and warm presence. "Wonderful stuff," he said. "Wonderful."

I then led a forty-five-minute session in which I first described a couple of meditation strategies and then led the group through them. The first strategy was the Inner Smile, giving kindness and care to your own body and feelings, and the second was around noticing subtle physical sensations of pleasure and then yielding to them. Toward the end of my talk, I admitted to the audience that I was uncertain about whether these techniques were of any use to someone who was coming out of a breakdown, depression, or psychosis.

"Not so," John spoke up clearly. "You can do this stuff even when you're really down."

There was then a discussion in which people spoke about the beginnings of recovery after a mental-health crisis. For all of them the most important moment was when a part of their mind woke up and they became conscious of their condition and could finally recognize that they needed to self-manage. That moment, they said, was crucial in the process of healing.

It was in this discussion that the idea of the one-brain-cell strategy emerged because, John explained, in the midst of his crisis, he needed only one of his brain cells to wake up to begin the process of self-management.

"In the middle of my worst depression, with voices in my head that I couldn't control, all I needed was just a tiny part of my mind to wake up and think with kindness about myself," said John. "Just one brain cell in the midst of all the chaos, feeling compassion for the rest of me. Just one tiny part of me, tuning into the beauty of nature and life. This is like a tiny candle in the vast darkness of a huge, black cave. Yes, it's a tiny light, but, without it, it's complete darkness."

A SPECK OF DUST WITH UNIVERSAL AWARENESS

In the midst of crisis, overwhelming circumstances, pain, and suffering, just one cell of consciousness can wake up, connect, and give compassion. I love the minimalism and the humility of this approach. It does not seek a grand solution. It does not need us to make a huge shift. We do not need to be in a state of full connection and total compassionate equanimity. Just one conscious cell can make a difference, giving us just enough detachment to begin the process of self-management.

The particular beauty for me in this approach is the relationship between the tiniest and the most unbelievably grand and immense.

Sometimes, of course, like all healthy human animals, we get pumped up with our own self-importance, but then—in the normal rhythm of expansion and containment—we deflate and maybe even collapse. We become small and unimportant, ignorant, and easily ignored. Wisely, we may then acknowledge that we are only tiny specks in the vast mystery of creation of billions of stars, of incomprehensible distances and dimensions.

And there is this miracle.

This tiny single cell within you, this minuscule speck of consciousness, through an act of spiritual connection and surrender, can come into rapport with the most sublime beauty and inspiration. With just one cell of awareness you can know that you are one with the whole natural world, dust and stardust, this instant and out into infinity. And, in that instant, the fulfillment of your potential to be wise and loving is fully experienced. A speck of dust with universal awareness.

At the beginning of this chapter I warned you that we were going to go into uncomfortable territory, and I hope I have caused no undue distress. One of the most redemptive features of our species is our capacity to develop compassion. I trust, therefore, that this exploration of spirituality's shadow and psychology provides a process that improves our experience of universal benevolence and develops our loving kindness.

Part Three

SERVICE

CHAPTER 5

BEING TRUE TO
YOUR HIGHEST VALUES

✳

Compassion. Kindness. Generosity. Justice. Freedom. Education. Equal rights.

Instinctively we know that these great virtues and ethics are entwined with spirituality. But, at the beginning of this book, I described how the new spirituality is often criticized for its tendency toward narcissism and quick-fix consumerism. My well-being. My success. My happiness. It can seem obsessed with developing the self and appear to have no concern for the wider community.

We know full well, however, that there is no use in developing our connection with the magic of life if it does not spill over to serve others. The essential proof of our developed hearts and expanded consciousness is surely our instinct for compassion and caring for others. And at the core, too, of the reflection and self-management that we explored in part 2 are consistent inquiries about our value and usefulness to the community of life. To be actively engaged in helping and supporting others is a fundamental part of spirituality. The new spirituality is therefore in unequivocal solidarity with all the great religious and philosophical traditions in asserting values, ethics, and being of service. The best-known authors and teachers associated with the new spirituality, such as Eckhart Tolle, continually remind us and inspire us to put love into action and not to be solo performers.[1] This third part of the book, then, is dedicated to the whole ethos of service and practical compassion. In this chapter we look first at how, aligned with the goodness and flow of life, we can clarify our values and then put them into action, especially in behaving more mindfully and benevolently in all our relationships and communications. Then, in the following chapter, we look at the more classical spiritual ways of benefiting the world, particularly the use of presence, prayer, and healing.

RELIGION PROVIDES MORAL GUIDANCE

To begin, it is certainly a challenge for us that the new spirituality is a child of the modern age and therefore individualistic. The heart of our spirituality rests in our personal spiritual experience, but this individualism, simply because it is so independent, can look selfish compared with the traditional faiths, which are embedded in our communities and have clearly communicated ethical codes.

The major religions, for example, pioneered education, medicine, and social justice. Temples, mosques, and churches were oases of peace, healing, and creativity in otherwise disturbed environments. Priests, priestesses, monks, and nuns showed the way in selfless caring for their fellows. Even today, if you were living on the streets or in danger, where might you first go for help and sanctuary? In no-go inner-city areas and terrible places of civil war, it is still the temples, mosques, and churches that provide shelters of humane decency.

All the great religious teachers and traditions also speak clearly about the ethical imperative to live a life of service: the Ten Commandments of Judaism, the Sermon on the Mount in Christianity, the Noble Eightfold Path of Buddhism. At their best, the great religions nurture and encourage goodness and generosity of spirit. In fact, for many people, ethical guidance may be the most important aspect of religion and spirituality. The ethics of compassion, caring for your neighbor, charity, and doing unto others as you would have them do unto you are at the core of all the world faiths. This is what believers of Christianity, Judaism, Islam, Buddhism, Hinduism, and Sikhism expect. When people are wrestling with ethical dilemmas, their religions provide clear moral guidance.

Traditional religions also provide great stories that deliver a meta-narrative about how we should live our lives. Moses, Jesus, Mohammed, Buddha, and Krishna—these holy men were all presented as supremely virtuous and gave clear ethical teachings; and their stories dominated their cultures. In today's world, which is increasingly filled with rapid change, consumerism, and information overload, it is just as crucial that we have the inspiration of values and ethics that are clearly communicated.

And here we have an immediate challenge. If the status and influence of traditional faiths is declining, where now will we find our ethical leadership?

CLARIFY YOUR VALUES

It is useful to understand these criticisms of the new spirituality, because they help clarify where we stand and where we will find ethical leadership. There is, first of all, the sharp criticism that the new spirituality provides no clear values. Then there is an even sharper criticism, which is that, because it is so modern and multicultural, people involved in the new spirituality are not actually capable of having any clear ethical ideas. We are too busy being modern and welcoming diversity.

We are being so careful to accept everyone's religious, spiritual, and ethical beliefs that we will accept almost any idea, lack discernment, and have forgotten how to choose between what is right and what is wrong. A good example of this might be how we protect women's rights in our own country, but, if we hear about abusive sexism in another country, we might tolerate it because "it's just their culture."

Also embarrassing is the fact that the new spirituality is sometimes so entwined with capitalism and consumerism that it seems to be selling material success as if it were a high value. Instead of promoting love, wisdom, generosity, compassion, self-sacrifice, and courage, the new spirituality can seem to be selling products that deliver perfect health, well-toned bodies, and temporary happiness.

To be clear, I of course support health and happiness, in the same way that I support clean air, education, and shelter for everyone; but they are not the end products or purpose of spirituality. The outcomes or expressions of spirituality are surely compassion and enlightenment, love and consciousness, dedicated to all.

This is precisely why the new spirituality must be as explicit and clear as the traditional faiths about its ethics. In a society full of chaos, temptation, and selfishness, one of the fundamental services provided by spirituality must be a clear statement about what is right and what is wrong. And if the ethical guidance of traditional faiths declines, we cannot allow a moral vacuum to appear.

The challenge, then, is a very personal one, directly posed at us. If the new spirituality is diverse and individualistic, if it has no central organization and hierarchy, then its statements about ethics and values must come from all of us as individuals.

This means therefore that it is important to know your values, live by them, and also communicate them. This starts with clarifying exactly what your values are, in the way that I had to clarify mine, as described in the introduction. I thought that, just because I was a nice guy and had led most of my life in education, caring, and social activism, my values were obvious. But they were not, and so I had to develop my own values statement, and I also worked with a group to write the values statement for the foundation where I work.

Since then, I have led many trainings for colleagues and students to help them clarify and express their own values. There is a wonderful breakthrough moment for many people as they contemplate, realize, and articulate what they really believe in and support.

One committed social activist and educator wrote to me after a training to express astonishment that she had never previously focused mindfully on her values. "Actually taking some time out to contemplate and recognize my values has given me a sense of great strength. I've remembered what really matters to me, and can now check that what I'm doing is congruent with those values. And I can communicate them now to others, which in turn inspires them."

I encourage you yourself to clarify your values. You have read the values statements in the introduction. You have explored your own connection with the wonder and energy of creation in part 1. You have paused and reflected on how best to guide the growth of your heart and consciousness in part 2, and now it is appropriate to clarify your own values.

EXERCISE
CLARIFY YOUR VALUES

Take a few minutes of quiet time and sink down into yourself.

Sink into the attitude of the Inner Smile, the exercise we have been using throughout the book, so that you have a kind attitude toward yourself and your own body.

Relax your stomach. Slowly and patiently, open your heart, soften your eyes, and guide yourself into having a kind mind.

Focus into your heart and be aware of your own tendency and instinct for love, compassion, and caring for others.

Be aware, too, of all the heartfelt values and ethics in all the world's great religious and philosophical traditions, reminding us to be generous, compassionate, and supportive.

Chapter 5

Ask yourself: What are my most cherished values? What ethics and values do I hold most dear? For what values do I feel a real passion?

Many possible words may pass through your heart and mind. Here are a few examples: *justice, freedom, love, equality, truth, community.*

Reflect on what values sit most deeply and passionately in you. This is a relaxed and contemplative process.

Then, when you are ready, complete this sentence: *The values that I support most passionately are . . .*

Allow this sentence to sit in your mind and in your heart. Repeat it to yourself several times as if it were a mantra or affirmation.

Allow this sentence also to sit deep in your abdomen, like a voice booming and echoing in a great cave. *The values that I support most passionately are . . .*

When you feel ready, come out of the exercise and write down your values.

You can repeat this exercise as many times as you like. Over the months and years, your sense of your values may change and grow.

When you have written down your values, you may want to place them on the wall or use them as a screensaver. You may also want to write them in the form of a statement. *My highest values are . . . .* Or, *My life is dedicated to . . .*

It is very helpful and supportive to be continually inspired by and reminded of our values. They nudge us into more benevolent behavior when we might otherwise be sucked back into more selfish or thoughtless actions. They also remind us of what we really believe and support, which can be truly encouraging when we face life crises or are looking, for example, at why perhaps we do not have more material success or status. Many of my students and colleagues have instinctively made clear life choices prioritizing their values over material wealth, but they were not conscious they had made these choices.

"Of course, you're not a billionaire," I reassure them. "You chose a life of care and working to help people."

But living according to our values, like everything else in this book, is always work in progress, as we endeavor to do our best.

COURAGE AND CHIVALRY

Doing our best, however, requires discipline and courage. We can see these two virtues in natural action when a mother protects her young. It would be a dereliction of her natural duty if she allowed her children to be harmed. History, too, is full of heroic men and women who have dared to risk their lives and fight for the freedom and rights of their fellow beings.

When working on an early draft of this book, I was inspired and touched by the example of Chesley Sullenberger, the pilot who landed his passenger airplane in the Hudson River after geese struck its engines. He was the first pilot ever to land a craft of that size, an Airbus 320, successfully on water. Then, after all the passengers and crew had escaped, and while the plane was sinking, he calmly walked up and down the fuselage twice—*twice*—to ensure no one was left behind, before he himself made his exit.

During this whole crisis, he behaved in a centered, mindful, and courageous way. He did his duty, and he did it with calm elegance. He was also impressive after the crash, when the incident became an international story and his skills and bravery were commented on across the world's media. He remained dignified and humble. He was honest and said that he had experienced "the worst sickening, pit-of-your-stomach, falling-through-the-floor feeling" that he could ever have imagined. When asked how he had dealt with that, he said that it was an act of "focus" and that he had to get on with the job for which he was trained.

Reflecting on the whole event, he said afterward that he realized something important and meaningful had sparked the public's attention and that he did not want to say or do anything to deflate that.

I liked his chivalry, his ability to be brave and emotionally considerate without any pomposity or bragging. He knew when to be courageous and a leader, and he knew when to be humble and quiet.[2]

Sometimes, however, people are reluctant to be seen and to make a stand. "I prefer to keep my beliefs to myself. And, if I do good, then that's for me to know—not broadcast it," one man said to me. "Spiritual people always prefer to keep quiet," another said. "Spirituality is about being internal, not external."

They also do not want to sound pompous or evangelical, or to look like priests in a pulpit or get into arguments and find themselves having to defend their position. They may often prefer to remain quiet, rather than risk an uncomfortable confrontation.

These feelings are understandable, but not good enough. There are crucial situations and issues that require clear action and a clear voice with clear values. Otherwise, we may passively collude with the selfishness, delusions, and injustices of society, simply by leaving them unchallenged. There is no virtue to sitting in meditation while someone is being abused and we can do something about it. There is no virtue in doing nothing or remaining silent while our fellows in humanity and nature are harmed by a social system and culture of which we are a part.

Confronting an abusive situation may be challenging, especially for those people who have high ideals and are committed to a life of service, but are timid. Yet we know that when someone or some living thing is being damaged or threatened, then action of some kind is needed. Sometimes it is courageous physical intervention. Other times it is speaking clearly.

There are no simple answers here, but we do know that every challenging situation is an opportunity for compassion, mindfulness, and reflection, discriminating about what would be of best service.

DOING GOOD IS A WAY OF CONNECTING

Living by your highest values and being of service create a loop that can benefit you too. My father, a Freudian psychiatrist, would have been very cynical about this. I remember his telling me to be careful about my do-gooding instincts. "There's always a hidden motive," he cautioned. "Self-gratification."

But I am not referring here to the smugness that can come from virtuous behavior. I am referring to a genuine benefit from doing good that can support our health and general well-being.[3] The spiritual perspective here is that when we do good, we behave in a way that is similar to the essential and benevolent nature of the cosmos. When we act with compassion, good humor, and generosity, we put ourselves into the same resonance as the cosmic flow. We are like tuning forks or the tuning dial on a radio or television. When we do good we are tuning in, putting ourselves on the same frequency as the loving beneficence that permeates creation. In the words of Saint Francis of Assisi, "It is in giving that we receive."

In one psychology experiment, for example, participants played an economic game in which they could donate some of their payment to another participant. Before and after each game, the participants' stress hormone, cortisol, was measured. Those who behaved selfishly had much higher stress levels, laying the foundations for increasing ill health and a low immune system, than those who were more generous.[4] This finding is part of an increasing body of research that demonstrates how kindness benefits the donor, supporting good health and even relieving depression. Acts of generosity, too, for example, can relieve melancholy and inertia, reconnecting us with life's vitality.[5]

Here is a story of service in action, which will help clarify how this all works.

For many years I lived next to great neighbors, Tony and Anna, who were unusually kind when my daughter, Sophie, was two years old. Her best friend was another toddler who lived in the house on the other side of Tony and Anna's garden. We all lived in a road that ran along a steep hill, and our homes were all twenty or more steps up through sloping gardens. So, for the toddlers to play together, one of the parents had always to walk or carry one of them down the garden, down the steps and along the road, up the steps, and so on. This could happen several times a day, pushed along by the two children shouting to each other across the gardens.

For several months Tony and Anna watched the two families walking back and forth. Then, without telling us, as a surprise and a gift for the children, they created two small gaps in the hedges on both sides of their garden and a small path across their lawn. For the next five years, until they were old enough to go alone on the road, the two children were able to cross Tony and Anna's garden to meet each other. It enhanced the lives of the two children, made the parents' lives much easier, and created a sense of community.

So, if you were to ask me where you might best be of service in your life, I would suggest that you might start by giving caring attention to your immediate neighbors. This message is not new, is it? Old Testament prophets and Jesus explicitly taught it when they said, "Love thy neighbor." Put into action, this means giving those people who live nearest to you the benefit of your thoughtfulness, even if minimally it means only greeting them with a smile of welcome, a wonderful small step in building a sense of safe community.

DOING GOOD IS PART OF THE UNIVERSAL FLOW

My neighbors were acting in a way that was congruent with a benevolent and free-flowing cosmos. They had a natural sense of when there is blockage and constraint, and a natural instinct to release and enable the flow and movement of life.

To release something from constriction is an instinctive act that supports movement and growth. We instinctively release a bird caught in a room or a child caught in pain or a whole caste of people caught in dire economic and social conditions. When we feed, house, educate, and respect people we release them from fear and anxiety into the conditions for growth and freedom. When we give people the conditions for happiness, well-being, and health, they can grow in heart and mind.

This instinct can be clearly seen in other animals. I have swum several times with dolphins, for example, and have experienced directly how they behave and relate to human beings. My understanding, along with that of other researchers, is that dolphins have a form of radar, which can sense whether another creature is tense or relaxed. When they perceive that a human being is tense, they know instinctively that this is contrary to the natural flow of nature and they then intervene to relieve the tension.

They therefore play and relate with great sensitivity, helping people to melt their physical and emotional tautness and rigidity. In one session that I experienced in a therapeutic dock in the Florida Keys, a small family of dolphins ignored me for a long time, and then the mother came to look in my eyes. I then felt a deep pain in my chest and then relaxed in a way I had never previously experienced. Using sonar vibration, she had "massaged' and melted tissue constriction around my heart and chest. I was startled, then grateful.[6]

I believe that we human beings help each other for similar reasons. We do not have the sonar-echoing abilities of dolphins, but we can empathically feel and notice where there is constriction. We then act instinctively to release it. This is a natural empathy for our fellow beings.

One contemporary author, Frans de Waal, professor of primate behavior at Emory University, has written extensively about the existence of seemingly moral behavior in nonhuman species and has in fact called for an age of empathy to balance and solve our global challenges. "It's not as though we're asking our species to do anything foreign to it," he writes. "Every individual is connected to something larger than itself. . . . The connection is deeply felt and no society can do without it."[7]

In the language of sociobiology, Professor de Waal is expressing a very basic spiritual insight. We *are* connected to everything: the event that birthed our cosmos, every star, every blade of grass, every creature and one another.[8]

Some people, it seems to me, are born with this natural empathy for other people, animals, and plants. They appear to come out of the womb with green fingers and a warm heart, able instinctively to understand and sense the plight and feelings of other beings. Others of us are not born with such lovingly attuned sensitivities, but the more that we learn to pause and mindfully yield to our connection with life's wonder, the more we seem naturally to develop an open heart and greater empathy. How can it be otherwise? As we connect more fully with spirit, we connect more fully with everything—and everyone.

AFFECTION AND CARE IN RELATIONSHIPS

In caring for everyone, we know that people need physical care: food, shelter, and safety. We also know that emotional care is just as crucial. Without emotional kindness, people wither and, at worst, become dangers to themselves and others. Without affection, the brains and nervous systems of children do not develop properly.[9]

The new spirituality, therefore, powerfully asserts the values of caring for each other with emotional sensitivity and affection.

Ultimately, this caring is surely what will transform human society and could create heaven on earth. Moods, attitudes, and good health can ripple through society "like pebbles thrown into a pond," wrote James H. Fowler and Nicholas A. Christakis in a *British Medical Journal* paper that examined the spread of happiness and its implications for individual and communal health over a twenty-year period with more than four thousand people.[10]

Increasing the general levels of happiness and well-being can, of course, be brought about by increased material wealth. But there are many studies describing poor societies that are rich in happiness and what is sometimes called "social wealth." Over and over again, anthropological research shows that indigenous peoples, sometimes living in great poverty, have a level of communal happiness that surpasses Western levels. This happiness is based in mutual care, sharing, and affection.[11]

Sadly, though, expressing care and affection to each other is so much easier advised than put into practice. We need to be realistic. In all our close emotional relationships, old psychological stuff such as resentments and trauma can be easily churned up, and we may find ourselves in ancient addictive and destructive behavior. Often in my trainings, I look at my companions and say, "What we're doing here in this class is not the real workshop or training. This is easy. The real training is at home in your closest relationships." Everyone always nods in wry agreement.

Home and the workplace are the major arenas in which we need to demonstrate our values through care and affection. It is not so difficult to buy ecologically sound cleaning products or to do good works in those situations where there is obvious suffering and need, but it is tough to be loving and emotionally generous with those whom we encounter all the time. It is most difficult to be centered and chivalrous when we are stuck in habitual grooves of behavior, especially in family, work, and intimate relationships. Especially in these daily circumstances, the essence of spiritual service, in the midst of all of

171

the usual provocations and trials, is that we remain centered, connected, reflective, and aligned with our highest values.

For ten years, I codirected London's major program of the new spirituality at St. James's Church, Piccadilly, hosting a new speaker every week. The speakers were all authors or teachers who were prominent in their fields, and I was able to speak with all of them backstage in a relaxed and collegial environment. Almost without exception, they agreed that the most difficult place to demonstrate our values and our spirituality was at home and in our closest emotional relationships.

"If you want to find out the truth about spiritual teachers," one of them said to me, "talk to our wives or husbands. They'll know if we practice mindfulness and loving kindness. If I can become more loving at home, then I know that I have really shifted."

Again, for those of us not born with the disposition of a kindly saint, this can be hard work. Throw me to the lions. Send me to work in the most dangerous shantytowns. But don't ask me to be patient and kind with my irritating children/partner/parent/colleague.

This area is precisely where being able to connect and reflect is so important. If every time you feel you want to behave negatively inside a close relationship you could just press the pause button—and, instead of being negative, focus yourself on a moment of connection with life's magic—wouldn't that be better?

This is where the one-brain-cell and Inner Smile strategies can be so helpful. One single brain cell remembers to connect, to be kind and forgiving. Especially if we are tired and overwhelmed, this kind of loving self-discipline can be tough. We also know that the bungee cords of resistance can suck us back into old behavior. But persistently practicing our connection with the wonder and energy, consistently being mindful and self-caring, and consistently remembering and aligning with our values will carry us through these difficult changes into being more consistently loving.

SEEING THE BEST IN OTHERS

From one perspective we could even suggest that the core theme of service in the new spirituality is good relations—good relations with nature, with the cosmos, and with each other. We need clearly to expand our understanding of values and service so that it not only includes the explicit areas of suffering, abuse, and injustice that require relief, but also fully incorporates how we behave in relationships.

We have already clearly asserted that all creatures on our planet need respect and care. We have noticed, too, that human beings also explicitly need affection if we are to develop healthily. But, having made these idealistic generalizations, we need to understand what these relationships look like in practice.

One of the fathers of the counseling and psychotherapy movement, Carl Rogers, had some specific and useful advice here. He suggested three core behaviors or conditions necessary for every good psychotherapist and counselor, regardless of psychological school or particular techniques. These behaviors are also directly relevant to all of us, because they create a respectful, protective, and affectionate environment in which true rapport and connection between people can take place; and it is in this rapport that people feel safe to heal, grow, develop, be creative, and fulfill their potential.

In his autobiography Carl Rogers remembered, "In my early professional years I was asking the question: How can I treat, or cure, or change this person? Now I would phrase the question in this way: How can I provide a relationship which this person may use for his own personal growth?"[12]

The three core behaviors he suggested are

- unconditional positive regard: always see the best in someone;

- empathic understanding: listen with complete attention and all your senses; and

- congruence: be authentic, real, and honest; be true to yourself.

This ability to see the best in someone and be present to them with all your senses can also be described in a more soulful language. Your soul, your core, is greeting and being present to their soul and all that they are. This is a wonderful way of meeting someone, requiring that we be mindful, connected, and centered.

How wonderful to meet the members of your family in this way, as well as your friends, neighbors, and colleagues. *I greet your soul.* This greeting, in fact, is a symbolic part of daily Hindu life. You meet someone, place your hands in a prayerful position in front of your heart or brow, and then bow to the person, saying, *"Namaste"* (I greet your soul). In other words, no matter what situation we are in or what social status we have, we greet each other's essence. In Christianity, this practice is known as greeting the Christ Within.

EXERCISE
GREETING SOMEONE'S SOUL

Pause and sink calmly into yourself.

Guide your attitude into an ambience of compassion and humility.

Contemplate for a while what you find most beautiful and wonderful about the natural world and the cosmos.

Contemplate the profound mystery of the beginning of the universe— and also the mystery of how infinite space is. How did it begin? How far does it extend?

And softly focus on the benevolence and positive energy that pervades it all.

When you are ready and calmly centered, bring into your awareness any person you know.

Imagine and sense that you are bowing to that person and greeting her or his soul.

I greet your soul.

Stay centered and open in your heart.

HONESTY AND HUMILITY

This meeting of souls, free of status and social illusion, needs also to be accompanied by an openness and honesty that is unusual in our culture. In leadership and teacher-training courses, particularly in spirituality, it is crucial that we break down the old undemocratic, pompous, and hierarchical structures of authority and power.

Spirituality and religion have a history too full of priests, teachers, and believers who assert they have a special status or are free of the usual human challenges and ambiguities. All across the world you can see clerics and followers asserting that they have found the truth and they are God's chosen ones. In Palestine and Israel, for example, there are Jews, Christians, and Muslims all demonstrating this behavior. You are also familiar, I imagine, with the cartoon character of the spiritually smug individual who is holier than thou and always knows best. Unfortunately, this caricature is based in reality.

This behavior in spiritual leaders is delusional, manipulative, and disempowering. Especially when people are awakening or in distressing circumstances, they are at their most vulnerable and need wise leadership.

The new spirituality, self-reflective and psychologically literate, therefore explicitly suggests that people who claim to be spiritual also be humble, truthful, and transparent about their own psychological and spiritual challenges. Especially in situations where we are talking about spirituality or where we have any status or authority, I recommend that we be willing to share about our own difficulties. We need to model transparent honesty and self-reflection. This echoes the way in which Christian and Buddhist monks are exhorted to be humble and approachable.[13]

Behaving in this open way levels the playing field and, in my experience, is always reassuring and encouraging for others. I am not suggesting that we advertise our failings indiscriminately, only that, where and when appropriate, we share our common travail. This humility and honesty can transform what has historically been an area of abuse and create relationships of mutual support and trust. Gratitude and forgiveness are also crucial attitudes here, and we shall discuss them in the next chapter.

BURNING OUT AND STAYING INSPIRED

Be careful, though, that in your service to others you do not exhaust yourself. Sadly, there are many genuine servers who are burning out and have lost their fuel. For example, I worked once with a team of senior nurses, all of whom were tired and cynical about their work. They were basically staying in their jobs, waiting for their pensions.

"Is there nothing good or inspiring in your work anymore?" I asked. "Are there no moments at all when you see a patient respond in a way that touches your heart or when you see a colleague behaving in a way that you find good and uplifting?" They were surprised and touched by the question. One by one, they admitted that they still had moments like that, but that they did not focus on them or value them. They just sped through them and got on with the next task.

They then talked for a while together about what had called them into nursing in the first place, and they were remorseful about having lost their original inspiration. They were like the vicars who had lost touch with the magic of Holy Communion. After further discussion, they acknowledged that it would be good, the next time a meaningful encounter happened—with a patient, for example, who touched their hearts or a colleague whose work was helpful and inspiring—to pause and fully appreciate the moment with gratitude and awareness. While doing their healing work, they could also mindfully support their well-being through connecting with spirit and allowing themselves to feel the benefit of their connection.

CARING FOR THE NATURAL WORLD

Always in difficult times, it is our connection with the essential goodness and miracle of creation that can give us comfort and encouragement. We find this comfort in the natural world, from a grain of sand out to the total mystery of our cosmos. For many of us, nature is our major source of spiritual connection. Saint Bernard of Clairvaux, founder of the Christian Order of the Knights Templar, said, "What I know of the divine science and Holy Scripture I learned in the woods and fields." The beauty of dawn and the movement of air and water can touch the most cynical and harshest of people.

It is this fundamental empathy and rapport that is surely the authentic source and motivation for our green and ecological values and for our instinct to nurture and protect the natural world. We receive the blessing and inspiration of our natural environment, and it is only fair that we return this gift with our own respect and affection.

Spiritual practice and compassionate awareness extend beyond our human companions. In shamanic, pagan, and tribal religions, it is basic courtesy to treat animals, plants, rocks, clouds, rivers, and all living things as our friends and our relatives.

It is mindless and harsh of us, then, to receive nature's blessing—and then abuse her, selfishly looking after the bits we like and disregarding the others. We might care for our own pets and plants and then completely ignore the suffering of the animals that give us meat and leather. We might care for our own health and beauty but give no awareness to the ecologically damaging agents we use for housecleaning.

I hope that in most of this book I have managed to avoid any earnest haranguing, but I feel myself coming close to it when it comes to mindfulness and care of our environment and planet. I had a good friend who was an ecological activist, and every time she visited our home she would assertively point out the household stuff that was unethical and polluting. I twitched as she fingered my bad habits.

My monkey mind and bungee cords of addiction wanted to keep on using the same old stuff I had used for years. But I needed to adjust and give awareness to the damage I was actually doing, so I was grateful for her reminders and gradually turned my bad habits around.

Our inspiration to care for the natural world derives from our being part of it. Dale Carnegie, possibly the most successful self-help author of all time—he wrote *How to Win Friends and Influence People*—suggested the simplest of strategies, which most of us do instinctively. "Close your eyes. You might try saying something like this: The sun is shining overhead. The sky is blue and sparkling. Nature is calm and in control of the world—and I, as nature's child, am in tune with the Universe."[14]

Or, as my friend the Slovenian sculptor and author Marco Pogacnik once poetically said to me, "Look at how beautifully and perfectly the earth prepared herself for us!"

YOUR FAMILY OF NATURE AND COSMOS

Take a few minutes to pause and center. Relax and allow yourself to sink down into your body.

Guide your attitude into one of having an open heart and a kind mind.

Turn your focus down into your body and be aware of its wonder and life—its heat, the pulse and flow of your blood, the rise and fall of your breath, the way your lungs absorb oxygen.

Contemplate and enjoy the reality that you yourself are a miracle of creation.

Contemplate, too, that your body is made up of the same atomic matter, the same stardust, that constitutes everything else in nature and the cosmos.

You are made of the same stuff as the stars, the minerals, the plants and animals.

Just feel and be aware of your connection with all of this, with the whole of your family.

Carefully look at how you live your life—clothes, food, heating, energy, transport. Calmly assess the impact you have on your environment.

Aligned with your highest values and compassionately respecting all nature, make some careful and conscious decisions about your habits and lifestyle.

This realization is very beautiful, isn't it? We live in a beautiful natural world and, if we choose to, we can also live in a beautiful way. When we are touched by someone's caring behavior, we may say that she or he is a beautiful soul, and this has nothing at all to do with superficial appearances or material success.

Doing good and being good are also not derived from some earnest attitude devoid of joy and good humor. As well as beauty, the natural world is filled with wildness and vitality. Sometimes therefore our acts of service may also be wild, courageous, and even revolutionary, as we release what is trapped—emotions, animals, plants, people—into freedom.

But, whether our service is done in a quiet or expansive way, we know that our spirituality needs to be grounded in real-life behavior that lovingly supports and serves all those around us. The growth of our heart and consciousness is not a purely private experience, but has to spill over to benefit everything beyond us.

In the coming chapter we now look at more subtle and spiritual ways in which we can serve.

CHAPTER 6

PRESENCE, PRAYER, AND HEALING

✴

I t is empowering to be clear about our values, to live our lives in accordance with them, and to be of service to those around us through acts of sharing, generosity, care, courage, and compassion. Yet in spirituality there is also another dimension to service that is more subtle, invisible, and metaphysical. It is concerned with the quality of our presence and the atmosphere we radiate.

When we are centered and heart focused, with an encouraging psychological attitude, we create a vibration that is supportive for those around us. And, when we are simultaneously connected to the benevolence of the cosmos, this vibration or aura is amplified.

Working consciously and deliberately with this invisible dimension has always been a fundamental part of spiritual service and is, in essence, what differentiates the work of a priest or shaman from the secular work of a social worker or medical doctor. The core of this invisible, priestly work is precisely to be a conscious conduit and radiator for the wonder and energy of creation, so that other people can feel it and connect more easily. This is an essential part of the work of any vicar, rabbi, imam, lama, priestess, or shaman—to generate an atmosphere that helps people come out of the stimulation and distractions of daily affairs and connect back with the benevolent flow of creation.

In public events such as services, ceremonies, and worship, this is their explicit function: to be a facilitator of the wonder and energy. Whatever their faith, whether they work in a church, temple, or grove, their ceremonies and blessings are intended to create a spiritual energy and ambience that support, heal, and inspire their congregations. The medicine men and women then also carry this blessing and ambience out into their pastoral work.

In the new spirituality this specialist metaphysical work is no longer the preserve of a few ordained men and women, but can be practiced by all of us. In this chapter, therefore, we look at the service we can do through our presence, prayer, and healing. I name them as if they were three different types of work, but in reality they often blend into one, as we shall discover.

THE TWO SECRETS OF VIBRATIONAL SERVICE

We can all be of service through presence, prayer, and healing, but we need to appreciate that this spiritual work is based in an idea that is only just becoming a part of Western mainstream thinking. This idea, held by the new spirituality and most Eastern and shamanic religions, is that we live in a vast field of energy and that vibrations and atmospheres can move like waves through this field, influencing us and being influenced by us.

You may already be familiar with the Eastern names given to the energy that flows in this field. In yoga you may have come across the term *prana*. In martial arts and tai chi, you may also have come across the word *qi* or *chi*.

Students of religion and anthropology will recognize this concept of a natural vitality and energy that suffuses the cosmos and natural world in many other traditions: aether (alchemy, Latin); *akasha* (Hindu); *asha* (Iranian); astral light (Theosophy); *awen* (Welsh); bliss fields (generic); cosmic ocean (generic); *elan vital* (vitalism); holy spirit/ghost (Christian); *ichor* (Greek); *inua* (Inuit); *ka* (Egyptian);

loong (Tibetan); *maban* (Australian Aboriginal); *mana* (Polynesian); *manitou* (Anishinabe); *numen* (Latin); *orenda* (Iroquois); *prana* (Hindu); presence (generic); *qi* (Taoist); *sakina* (Islam); *seid* (Norse); *shekinah* (Jewish); *teotl* (Aztec); *väki* (Finnish).[1]

Historically, in the West in Christianity, Judaism, and Islam, discussion of this energy field and how to cooperate with it was discouraged as being dangerous. It was even thought, for example by the Catholic Inquisitors of the thirteenth century, to be the devil's work. There is still very little open conversation in traditional religions about the invisible mechanics of precisely how a priest's blessing works or why worship can so dramatically change the atmosphere from the mundane to something more special and blessed.

The sacred mechanics—connect and radiate—are not discussed or explicit. They are just part of God's mysteries. Nevertheless, even though not discussed, this field is always clearly being utilized in any religious ceremony or ritual, the performance of which is restricted to ordained clergy. In the past, and even today, anyone else performing ceremonies or working with energy is usually viewed as a blasphemous or dangerous competitor, possibly condemned and punished as a witch, Satanist, or pagan. Despite this oppression, throughout the centuries there have been secret groups, such as the Knights Templar or the Rosicrucians, who have studied metaphysics, the energy field, how we are influenced by it, and how we, in turn, can use and influence it.[2]

At the heart of these esoteric schools were two great secrets, which today are hardly secrets at all. The first secret was that the solid world we can see and touch is not all there is. The material world is just the tip of an iceberg and, in fact, we all live in and are part of a great ocean of vitality, energy, and consciousness that underlies and influences everything in existence. The second great secret was that, consciously or unconsciously, our thoughts, feelings, and actions can influence and cooperate with this vitality, energy, and consciousness. We affect the world through our mood and vibration.

This knowledge—that the world, including us, is made of energy and that we can influence it—was considered dangerous if placed in the wrong hands, because it was thought that selfish and unscrupulous people could use this information to manipulate others and dominate them. Until the last century, these secrets were only ever taught clandestinely to small groups and to students who were assessed as being trustworthy and guided by the highest values. The use of this metaphysical technology in healing was also only ever shared in secret and passed on from healer to healer. Equally, the energy techniques in yoga and martial arts were never taught in public classes, but were always restricted to trusted students.

Today, these secrets are a normal and accepted part of the new spirituality. They are, for example, at the heart of all the many different schools of spiritual healing, such as reiki.[3] Many people also know, for instance, the basic vitalizing strategies of yoga and martial-arts breathing.

The fact that modern science does not have a model for describing or explaining these effects is something we can wait for, though it could possibly all be understood through theories similar to those of radio broadcasting and wavelengths. The Pythagorean school of ancient Greece, for instance, taught its students that we all live in a cosmos of sound, vibration, and harmonics and that we ourselves are instruments that make vibrations. By changing our note and frequency, by changing our mood and the quality of our thinking, we affect the vibration in the wave fields around us, and this, in turn, affects the people around us.[4]

From one perspective, all this stuff about metaphysics and vibrations is a completely normal aspect of everyday life, because we all know how it feels when someone comes home or into the workplace in a bad mood: it is oppressive and depressing and affects us. Or how it feels when someone happy comes into our space: the effect is positive and enjoyable.

When we are calm, we radiate a calm vibration that other people can sense. When we look after someone with consideration and love, we radiate those beneficial qualities. Our negative moods have the opposite effect. This is all obvious. We unconsciously influence atmospheres all the time. We human beings are not just dense physical bodies. We are also consciousness, energy, electromagnetism, and metaphysical stuff that science does not fully understand.

The new spirituality is open and explicit about the metaphysical dimension of our lives, encouraging everyone to understand its basic logic and cooperate responsibly. It underlies a basic ethical imperative of spiritual service, which is to maintain your good humor. Whatever the situation, a basic act of service is to come home to your center, connect, practice kind watchfulness, and radiate a good vibration. Do not psychically pollute, but bless, your environment.

MY FAVORITE TEACHERS: GOOD PEOPLE

Over the years I have met many people who are relaxed in their bodies and connected to the benevolence of the cosmos, even if they may not be consciously aware of it. These are good people to have as our companions, especially in times of difficulty and crisis. In hospitals, for example, the people who often carry the most healing ambience are the porters, cleaners, and support staff. They are not speeding, nor overwhelmed with administration, but calmly doing their jobs and calmly comforting those around them. I often think of a woman I met in one of my earliest office jobs. She was the tea lady, pushing her trolley along between the desks, dispensing warm drinks and a warm attitude. Whenever she appeared, tensions would melt. She was grounded and centered in her body, and her heart and general attitude were generous and patient.

People like this quite often have a conscious spiritual connection, whatever language they might use to express it. I remember one

Jamaican carer who said with a smile, "I know that Jesus is always at my side." And I know an Irish pagan social worker who exudes a good vibration and is very clear. "Aye, I can always feel the background beat of the goddess's heart."

This calm and quiet sense of connection has been echoed by Christian orders whose monks and priests are dedicated not to being evangelical or trying to convert people, but just to living by example and radiating the presence of a loving Christ. This practice is paralleled among Buddhist monks who have taken the Bodhisattva vows of compassion and Muslim Sufi mystics who live invisibly in their communities, simply being a healing presence.

This practice is at the heart, too, of the martial-arts and Samurai traditions, in the concept of being grounded and in one's *hara*. *Hara*, you may remember from chapter 2, is the core skill of being grounded and embodied; it is the sense of being fully in your body and with your center of gravity down in your lower abdomen, similar to having a good "bottom" in horse riding. This stability then provides the foundation for a strong heart and generous mind. The greatest martial artists and Samurai have such an aura of chivalry and beneficence that the violent attitudes of other people are disarmed and melt away.

Over the decades, watching, listening to, and being in the presence of hundreds of spiritual teachers, I have found that I remember and value them most according to the quality of their presence. I always like being mentally stimulated and emotionally challenged for my development, but when I remember those people who have had the most influence on me, it is always those who were most connected and congruent with the wonder and benevolence of the cosmos. Their presence and radiation encouraged me.

I particularly remember hosting an event at St. James's Church, Piccadilly, for the Vietnamese Buddhist monk, activist, and poet Thich Nhat Hanh and being with him afterward in the vestry. He had just spent two hours talking to a thousand people and was calm and completely present. When some children came into the room, he noticed them immediately, paused, and crouched to make soft contact with them. Before he left the church that evening, he looked me in the eyes to check that all was well. "Anything else?" his eyes asked. Like a child, I asked this wonderful poet and teacher, who had seen so much suffering and was so deeply connected, for a hug, an embrace. "Of course," he said. Being embraced by him was like being enfolded in the silken wings of a butterfly.

I had a similar good experience with William Johnston, the Jesuit priest and author of many inspiring books, including his classic on meditation, *Silent Music*.[5] His presence soothed and supported me.

What I am describing in this section are people who are inherently good. When they pass through our lives and we then remember them, they leave an imprint and memory that is reassuring and benevolent, an inspiration we can emulate. In many ways I believe that being a comforting and healing presence is perhaps the greatest gift of service we can consistently bring to the world, the greatest proof of our spiritual genuineness.

THE GIFT OF A KIND AND MINDFUL PRESENCE

At its most fundamental, metaphysical service is about emanating a comforting and supportive presence to our families, neighbors, colleagues, friends, and whomever we happen to meet in our daily lives. You will know when you have mastered this because, when faced with crises and irritating situations, such as arriving home tired to find pots that need washing in the sink, instead of reacting or getting irked you will automatically sink into a centered, connected and healing attitude. Your Inner Smile of compassion will soothe any of your own ruffled feathers, and your presence will bless those around you.

A wonderful story that illustrates precisely how to develop this attitude is told by Gerda Boyesen, founder of biodynamic psychotherapy, an approach that integrates the psychological and physiological, and recognizes how trauma and incomplete states of arousal are remembered in both the mind and the tissue of the body. She describes how she developed this quality of being a supportive presence in her professional work almost by accident. In 1969, when she left Norway to set up a practice in London, her reputation preceded her and she immediately had a queue of clients. But all was not well.

> When I first came to London [she explained in an autobiographical essay], my English was not very good and I didn't always understand everything my patients were saying. So sometimes I asked them. And they got very irritated. . . . So, when I didn't understand what a patient was saying, I made myself very comfortable, and was sitting more and more relaxed. I just said, "Hmmmm-mmm. Yes, hmmm, continue." And suddenly my patients spoke more than they had ever spoken before. I just listened. And before I knew it, the patients had reached deep emotions, deep regression, deep understanding.[6]

Unable to follow what was being said by her patients, instead of becoming anxious Gerda chose to relax into temporary unknowing and be just a comforting and listening presence, trusting the flow of the situation. As an experienced body therapist, she was very familiar with the skill of relaxing her tissue and sinking into a state of deep relaxation and connection. Her body then radiated this connected and beneficent quality, and her patients, therefore, found themselves in the company of someone who was a deeply comforting and healing presence. The result was that they felt safe and encouraged and were able to open up more therapeutically.

In the last chapter we discussed that what really matters in therapy, and also in loving relationships, is the quality and presence of the therapist, which, to repeat, is often taught as being based in three core behaviors: always see the best in someone; always listen with complete attention; always be true to yourself. To these three, Gerda Boyesen clearly added a fourth, which is to be relaxed in your body and connected to the benevolence of the universe and to allow your benevolent presence to reassure and "hold" your companion.

THE SKILL OF "HOLDING" A SITUATION

This ability to be a reassuring and healing presence is not restricted to spiritual people or even kind people. We have all seen the toughest of men and women change their attitude and vibration as they cradle and reassure a hurt child. Without necessarily having any conscious awareness of what you are doing, you too will have sometimes, or often, cared for someone in this way. It is a natural and instinctive human skill, to be a reassuring presence when someone is vulnerable and needs support.

Some people are able to hold this reassuring ambience as an ongoing part of their character. It is one of the core skills practiced by good team leaders. Many of us can go into a school, hospital, or business, for example, and know almost immediately whether the leadership of that organization is connected, grounded, and supportive, because there will be a calm atmosphere running through the whole organization.

By calm I do not mean that these leaders are immobile or passive, or that the organizations are dull and lacking creativity. They can be hugely busy and productive, but permeating the activity there is a calm, grounded presence that is watchful and reassuring.

To be clear, some of this calming influence comes from appropriate body language and careful communications, but there is something metaphysical at play here too. The best communication skills in the world are meaningless if they are delivered with a vibration that is frigid and disconnected. These calm and creative organizations have leaders and managers who maintain connection and goodwill.

This atmosphere of calm and safety can be strengthened by consciously using the strategy of "holding," in which you take responsibility for the spiritual atmosphere and emotional tone of a situation.

The word *holding* is borrowed here from counseling, where it is said that good therapists "hold" their clients. Good parents also hold their children and good leaders hold their teams.

In tribal situations where the whole community may come together to discuss a crucial issue, there are elders in the clan whose major role is simply to hold the space. Their task is to keep the ambience safe, protected, and contained. No matter how heated the debate, these elders maintain their calm center of goodwill and deliberately radiate this calm around the space.

Again, this behavior is often instinctive, and you may have experienced it when caring for someone in distress. It is as if your heart is opening and expanding to comfort and hold your distressed companion.

Exercise

HOLDING THE SITUATION

Pause and sink into yourself. Allow your abdomen to sink in a relaxed way.

Guide your attitude into the Inner Smile, scanning your body and sending friendly messages down into it.

Softly allow yourself to feel the hum of connection. It is always there. Yield to its sensation. Sense it within you.

When you feel completely centered, stable, and connected, open your heart and awareness to your situation and its people.

Stay very relaxed and anchored into your body, breathing calmly, watching with compassionate equanimity.

From your lower torso and your heart, allow a warm and calm radiance to expand from you and encircle the situation, like soft wings extending outward and around.

Stay still, anchored, and good-humored. Your reassuring magnetism creates calm energy in which people feel safe. You are like a strong, well-rooted tree.

Maintain this stability and this holding for as long as you choose.

It is possible to practice holding in a prepared, conscious, and mindful way. Imagine that you are going to a business meeting or a family reunion where you know there may be some challenges. Imagine, then, that you go into this meeting having programmed yourself to stay centered, connected, and radiating a good energy that encompasses and holds the situation. Then, when you are actually in the situation, you remain centered, connected, and holding. This can dramatically help and influence the situation.

Good people, with patient and generous mindfulness, also hold irritating situations in everyday life. Imagine, for example, being in a post office, in a queue that is moving slowly and with people getting increasingly frustrated. Instead of joining in with the feelings of irritability, you use the situation as an opportunity for spiritual service. You come to center, connect with the wonder of life, and benevolently radiate a holding presence.[7]

Doing spiritual practice in a shop queue may seem unexciting, but surely this is precisely the kind of daily situation where it is most needed and where we might most easily forget to do it. This situation is precisely where the generosity of our goodwill can ripple out and be beneficial.

Chapter 6

QUIETLY HEALING THE PLANET

If you want, you can also turn up the volume and deliberately radiate a good atmosphere. I currently live in the west of England, in the small town of Glastonbury, at the center of which are the ruins of the abbey. This was once the largest center of Christian worship in Europe and at the height of its powers was a nonstop prayer machine, with a daily rhythm that began at three in the morning. The prayers, choral music, and chanting; the meditative walking in cloisters; the contemplative atmosphere used for copying sacred manuscripts or medicinal herb gardening—all of this was done to connect and radiate a blessing.

Some people look at the monasteries, abbeys, and convents of the world's religions and see only men and women unable to cope with the world, escaping reality. Others of us, understanding the metaphysical dynamics, see men and women whose lives are devoted to radiating a blessing.

Many of us living in the modern world also feel called to be of metaphysical service through meditation and prayer. But we do not have the social and cultural support of a residential spiritual community, so we need to develop our own rhythm of quiet healing that radiates out to serve the world. Aligned fully with our highest values, this kind of practice can bring us a growing sense of integrity, personal stability, and connection, as we take regular time to center and then, contemplating the world and its problems, allow a soft radiance and kind thoughts to go out to where they are needed.

We need to clarify here what we mean by prayer, because in this context we are not discussing a contemplative conversation with God or requesting some kind of help for ourselves. We are specifically discussing what might be called healing prayer. At the heart of healing prayer is the strategy we have discussed in previous chapters, of connecting with the field and then yielding to the experience, allowing the energy to come into you as though into a vessel that is open to receiving. But, instead of absorbing the blessing yourself, you then sense and guide it, using your imagination, to go beyond you to where it is needed.

When I was in my twenties and first exploring this area, I was suspicious of organized religion and the church, but I met a priest who showed me how this healing work was at the very center of Christian worship. He taught me how the most important of all Christian prayers, the Lord's Prayer, can be experienced as an act of service and healing.

The Lord's Prayer

Our Father which art in heaven,
Hallowed be thy name. [*Connect with the field*]
Thy kingdom come.
Thy will be done in earth, as it is in heaven.
[*Allow the connection to be felt in your body*]
Give us this day our daily bread.
And forgive us our trespasses [*Yield to the blessing*],
as we forgive those who trespass against us.
[*Radiate the blessing out to others*]
And lead us not into temptation, but deliver us from evil.
[*Open up more fully to the blessing so that it supports your values*]
For thine is the kingdom, and the power, and the glory,
for ever and ever.
Amen.
[*Affirm that you are connected with the wonder and energy and that it is
grounded fully in you*]

DISTANT HEALING

In a very real and beautiful way, when we are connected to the wonder and energy of creation and yielding to the subtle sensations of this connection, we are natural healers. This vibration of calm benevolence then radiates into the world.

In terms of the actual technique, it is extremely important to do healing work only when we are in a state of complete calm and with no intensity or emotion. If you are tense or aroused, then tension and arousal are what you will radiate, instead of the balm of peace. What follows now is an exercise that integrates best practice from many different traditions.

EXERCISE
SENDING HEALING TO OTHERS

Take a few minutes to sink down comfortably into yourself.

You may, in fact, already be in that state, sitting or lying somewhere.

Softly guide your attitude into the Inner Smile.

Then recognize that, just because you are alive, you are connected to the wonder and beauty of all creation. It is around you and it is in you. Perhaps you can sense its soft background hum. Perhaps you can feel it more strongly.

Yield and surrender to the subtle sensations and feelings of your connection.

With a relaxed and warm heart, allow your awareness to expand outward into your room, knowing that your vibration and ambience is benevolently affecting its atmosphere.

Then allow your awareness to move outward to wherever you sense healing may be needed. Think of that situation with compassion and heartfelt kindness. Be aware of it with an attitude of tenderness. Simply giving it awareness is enough to guide and send healing into the situation.

Be careful not to tense up at all. Regularly check that your breath is soft and relaxed and that you are sunk down into your center and your body. Just sit steady, calm, relaxed, and compassionate.

Hold the compassionate awareness for as long as you feel is comfortable.

When you have done it for long enough, slowly withdraw attention from the situation and bring your focus home to your own body.

Sink back into your body and scan yourself with your Inner Smile. Allow yourself to feel and absorb your connection with spirit.

Stay centered in this way until you feel completely at home in yourself.

Done day by day, patiently and persistently, this form of meditative healing can become a habitual groove that is good for you and very good for the world around you. How different the world might be if, in every street and every apartment block, there were people regularly doing this kind of metaphysical service.

STAYING CENTERED WITH CHILDREN

Sometimes parents and teachers ask me how they might be able to teach this healing awareness to children, and I reply that I am always cautious around the topic of spirituality and children, because I feel that children are free spirits and exuberant new energy. They are a natural force, like a bubbling spring or waterfall. Teaching them to be mindful is like herding cats.

But this issue raises a far more interesting insight for all of us, which can guide our own spirituality and how it manifests in real daily life. The reality is surely that the only people who can authentically teach children how to be compassionately centered are people who are already modeling it.

There is an example that helps illustrate this and that, when I share it in my classes, makes many people uncomfortable and then embarrassed—and then they smile with insight.

Think of the most precious object you may have in your home or office. It might be a piece of china or a painting or a smart phone or a laptop computer. Imagine, then, that a toddler, two years old and exploring, comes into the room and accidentally breaks, spills sticky juice on, or permanently defaces this favorite object. Your best vase breaks. Your television is ruined. I have known toddlers to place DVDs into toasters and biscuits into the DVD slot on computers; to use bright paints on virgin-white carpets; to dismantle flower arrangements; and so on.

You then come into the room and find the scene of destruction. One of your most precious belongings is destroyed. Do you calmly notice what has happened and smile with compassionate equanimity, concerned that the child is not frightened and feels loved? Do you kneel down to check that the toddler is all right? Do you calmly clean up the mess in a relaxed and unbothered way?

Or, if you feel a pang of loss and a rising anger, do you have the self-control to press your pause button, relax your stomach, switch on your Inner Smile, and stay connected?

Exploring this topic in class, I have seen people gasp. My favorite object! The child needs discipline! But it was a toddler and it was a mistake. And it was only a material object. Why disconnect and lose your temper and teach that child impatience and materialism?

Our spirituality does not stop when something happens that we dislike.

TRANSFORMING NEGATIVE ENERGY

When adults stay centered and compassionate, behaving with emotional generosity and grace after seeing or experiencing something they dislike, they may feel that they are having to "eat" their own angry and hurt reactions. Metaphysically and spiritually, this is an act of great service. Be clear, though, that I am not suggesting you absorb or collude with abuse or bullying.

Eating our own bad mood so that it does not pollute others is an act of chivalry and healing. It is also an act of self-discipline, because in those moments when we become aware that we are about to lose our temper or behave badly, and we press the pause button to deliberately alter our behavior, it can hurt. It is as if there were brakes screeching inside us, as we stop the momentum of rising adrenaline and bring it under control. At the same time, we are transmuting negative emotion and energy into something more positive and beneficial.

The more we transform our own negativity, the less we pollute the world around us. If we envisage the world as a single interconnected energy system, then, when we eat our own negative energy and replace it with benevolence, we are adding something positive to the sum total for everyone.

But, of course, this needs to be done with emotional intelligence, lest we end up sitting on a simmering backlog of resentment and anger, so it needs to be supported by our connection with the benevolence and wonder of creation and with honest and good-humored reflection.

This ability to absorb and transmute negativity is not just something that we can do with our own emotions and energy. There is also a spiritual practice, taught in several traditions, of absorbing and transmuting the negativity and pollution created by others. It is specifically taught, for example, in Tibetan Buddhism and known as the practice of *Tonglen*, Tibetan for "giving and taking." This strategy is said to have been originally taught by the eleventh-century Indian

Buddhist Atisha Dipankara Shrijnana and has become better known recently because the current Dalai Lama says that it is part of his daily spiritual practice, which starts with his waking at 3:30 a.m. and then prayers, meditating, and reading holy texts, with a short break for walking and breakfast, until his lunch at noon.[8]

This practice is also at the heart of metaphysical Christian service, the ability to turn the other cheek and absorb the negativity of those around you, its supreme symbol being the act of sacrifice embodied by Jesus on the cross, absorbing and redeeming negativity for all humanity.

It is something also that you may have already experienced in your own life. You may, for example, have cradled and held someone weeping with distress and felt as if you yourself were absorbing the distress. From an energetic perspective, this is indeed exactly what was happening. You were absorbing negative vibrations. Through instinctive warmth, generosity, and love, you were holding, melting, and transforming them.

EXERCISE
BREATHE IN NEGATIVITY, BREATHE OUT BLESSING

This is a powerful practice so do it only when you feel psychologically stable and strong—and you have a clear instinct and intuition that it feels healthy and appropriate for you to practice it. Do not do this exercise if you are tired, unhealthy, or feeling at all vulnerable or overwhelmed by life.

Absorbing and transmuting negative energy is practiced only from the foundation of a deep, grounded, and connected state of meditation and prayerfulness.

Take some silent time where you can be still and undisturbed.

Allow yourself to sink into your center and into your connection with the unconditional compassion that is embedded in the cosmos.

Make sure that your experience of the benevolence of creation is so great that you are soaking in it and fully connected.

From this safe and connected attitude, you then slowly become aware of the suffering and pain endured by so many in our world. You can sense and imagine it as a dark cloud.

With care and mindfulness, you then inhale some of this suffering and negativity, perhaps visualizing it as a very small amount of dark vapor.

This negative energy is breathed into your heart and stomach regions, and held there. This may feel uncomfortable. You hold it with your attitude of the Inner Smile, supported by the benevolence of your cosmic connection.

You then visualize, sense, feel, or imagine this negative energy transforming into something benevolent. You absorb and transform this tiny amount of negativity. With compassion and care you cradle it, love it, accept, and melt it into something new.

You then breathe out an energy of love, compassion, and blessing.

Finding your own rhythm, you breathe in negativity, you breathe out blessing.

This work is always done with great serenity. If, at any time, you feel the beginnings of any anxiety, then slow down and back away from it, sinking into your cosmic connection with unconditional love.

At the end of the exercise, bring your full attention back to your body and check that you feel fine.

If you feel any stuff "stuck" to you, go out into fresh air and move your body so as to release it.

And I repeat: as a health-and-safety caution, do not do this exercise when you feel tired or vulnerable or have an instinct that it may not be appropriate for you.

FORGIVENESS

This ability to stay connected, absorb, and voluntarily transmute harmful atmospheres is also the foundation of authentic spiritual apology and forgiveness. They are not just communications; they are also deep emotional and metaphysical shifts as we take what were previously negative energies and atmospheres and transform them into blessing.

When we center, connect, and yield to the subtle sensations of the benevolent field, we are in one way just tiny specks remembering our true context. Here we all are, miniscule and on this tiny planet in an incomprehensibly vast and beautiful universe. There is nothing any of us can ever do that will affect the flow and goodness of the cosmic ocean.

Of course, I know full well that we do harmful, sometimes terrible, things, but, placed within the cosmic context, we can do nothing to affect the great flows and movements out of which, for instance, galaxies emerge and then recede. The cosmic flow, the universal love, does not stop because one of us has been bad.

So when we open to connection, whether it is a glorious moment on a mountain or whether it is melancholic and curled up under the duvet, we allow the flow and the benevolence into us, regardless of whether we have been good or bad. Whatever we may have done, we are never separate from the universe out of which we are born. And so, within this context, the universe is in a state of perpetual and graceful forgiveness, taking no notice of our ill doings or our guilt and shame. Its beneficence and flux do not halt because of our bad behavior.

It is because of this that mystics have always asserted that deity is, by its very nature, unconditionally forgiving. When, therefore, you are reflecting on your behavior and attitudes and contemplate your possible harmfulness or inadequacies, never feel unworthy or unforgiven. So many of my students and colleagues, when doing self-reflection, have told me they feel unworthy to receive and have spiritual experience.

"I'm not worthy to connect with cosmic love. My consciousness is too primitive. I'm such an idiot and have done such stupid things," one friend said to me.

But this is to project onto the great mystery of the cosmos that it is somehow like an admonishing parent or schoolteacher with limits to its patience and care. That is not the nature of the great mystery of the cosmic ocean.

Similarly, the whole nature of the Inner Smile, as we focus kindly down into our bodies and feelings, is a form of self-acceptance and self-forgiveness. A harsh and judgmental mind does no good to anyone, only creating more harm as it takes us into tension and separates us from connection.

So it is, of course, that all across the world we find a large variety of prayers and meditation practices that develop our awareness of forgiveness, both within ourselves and in the cosmos. I have already quoted the Lord's Prayer, where forgiveness appears at the heart of Christianity: "And forgive us our trespasses, as we forgive those who trespass against us." In all the major world religions, forgiveness sits, too, at the heart of their high ideals and values—to the self and to others.

Chapter 6

MEDITATION OF APOLOGY AND FORGIVENESS

Metaphysically, we can also use apology and forgiveness as a form of prayer and meditation that extends far beyond our direct personal circumstances. In my experience, it is best expressed in the Polynesian healing strategy known as *ho'oponopono*. One of its current teachers is Dr. Ihaleakala Hew Len, an educational psychologist in the United States.[9] I was inspired when I heard him in a presentation describe how the moment he received a phone call from a school, asking him to come in and help, he would immediately start to say the forgiveness prayer.

It is suggested that this prayer is effective because, somehow or another, we are all connected with absolutely everything in the cosmos and on this planet. So whatever events turn up in our lives, good or bad, we are somehow or another already connected with them, including their original causes. At a practical level for Dr Hew Len, this meant that when a school phoned with a problem and asked for his help his very first thought was that, in a metaphysical way, he was somehow both connected to and responsible for that problem. So he would immediately, silently, start saying the Ho'oponopono Prayer of Apology.

The Ho'oponopono Prayer of Apology

This is my responsibility.
I am sorry.
Forgive me.
Everything is love.
Thank you.

The prayer is wonderfully direct. It demonstrates spiritual courage and generosity. It absolutely trusts the oceanic field of benevolence. It is pure chivalry in its highest form. It is the polar opposite of psychological denial. It is the epitome of compassion and service.

202

In the acceptance of responsibility, there is no implication of guilt or shame or blame. It is just a simple truth about our relationship with the circumstances.

In my own life, this is the prayer I use the most often. Particularly when I am triggered, judgmental, or angry about someone or something, I will start to say this prayer. Years ago, for example, I found myself continually losing my temper with a difficult teenager, taking no responsibility for my own anger. One day, as I was about to lose my temper again, I had a blessed moment of mindfulness and realized that I truly had to take responsibility for what was happening and my own attitudinal violence. I walked away from the situation and began, silently, to say the prayer of apology. It brought healing and grace into me, and then, responsible and caring, I could in turn bring healing into the whole relationship.

This prayer leaves no room for the monkey mind to create a confabulating rationalization and story of avoidance. It cuts through any tendency to cling to habitual attitudes. It eats negativity and connects so as to bestow a blessing. It is wonderfully congruent with the Christian message of service and the Buddhist vows of service and compassion. It also sits at the heart of Muslim charity and Jewish righteousness.

It surrenders us immediately into the mature dignity of accepting unconditional responsibility. It is also filled with humility and implicitly trusts the power of universal benevolence to transform and heal all suffering.

EXERCISE
APOLOGY AND FORGIVENESS

Pause and go deep into your connection.

Bring into your awareness any work or family situation where there is conflict and where perhaps you have a tendency to apportion blame.

Greet the souls of the people involved and then with sincerity say the prayer:

This is my responsibility—I am sorry—Forgive me—Everything is love—Thank you.

IN GIVING WE RECEIVE

As I look back on the key spiritual experiences of my own life, I can see many important moments, but I wonder sometimes if any of them was as important as an experience in my very first school. In the playground one day I saw a girl with thick-lensed spectacles weeping while she was surrounded by children teasing her. In that single moment, a heartfelt fury and poignancy arose within me, a deep instinct that this was not fair, that she needed care and support. It was a raw emotion of compassion that woke within me and seems to have guided my life. Can I live my life in a way that is congruent with that compassion?

There is something about the passion of our hearts I do not fully comprehend, but that is all right because it is not an intellectual issue. In the way that a loyal dog may mourn the death of its owner, returning over and over again to a familiar place, so we humans are also capable of a sentiment that is filled with an instinctive loyalty and care for each other and for all life.

Our ability to love and care and be compassionate is an immense and wonderful gift. Earlier, in chapter 5, I quoted Saint Francis of Assisi: "It is in giving that we receive." And, in part 1, on connection, we looked at the very many different circumstances in which we most easily connect with creation's wonder and energy.

For many of us it may well be that it is when our hearts are triggered with compassion that we feel most deeply connected.

This then surely is the ultimate integration of our human spirituality—through the practices of connection, reflection, and service, we become increasingly conscious beings of compassion, filled with creativity, awe, and gratitude.

THE EXTRA DIMENSION

✳

In *The Spirit of the Child*, an important work of research that examines children's spirituality, there is a wonderful quotation from a young child, Ruth, describing heaven.

A mist of perfume, with gold walls, and a rainbow stretched over God's throne . . . but a transparent mist, like a . . . I can't explain it. Like a smell. A real cloud of smell, a lovely smell . . . like the smell that you get when you wake up on a dull winter morning, and then when you go to sleep, and you wake up, the birds are chirping, and the last drops of snow are melting away, and the treetops, shimmering in the breeze, and it's a spring morning. . . . I suppose it's not a season at all, not really because it's just a day in delight, every day.[1]

This child has an instinctive way with words and is able to communicate in joyous innocence, every sense alive, her connection with the wonder of life. Perhaps only a child could have spoken this beautiful description. Can you remember when you too had that enveloping awareness, filled with natural magic and exhilaration? Can you remember when you lost it? Perhaps you never did lose it. Perhaps you are one of those people who have always remained present to the wonder and energy.

And, if you did lose your connection, then no doubt you have regained it or are in the process of reclaiming it, or else why would you be exploring spirituality at all? This reclaiming can happen at any age.

My most enchanting meeting with such reclamation was with a couple I met while writing this book. He was ninety-one and she was eighty-five, and they had been married for fifteen years. He had been a science teacher and a committed atheist, while she had been a head teacher and a committed evangelical Christian since her early childhood.

After their retirement from work, however, as they separately relaxed and began to explore life more fully, they had each realized that, in their own words, they had allowed themselves to be brainwashed. They then found that there was a magic, a depth, and a diversity to life that was to be savored; and they were now enjoying their shared journey, participating in courses and experiencing different spiritual paths and approaches.

Their language was more considered than that of the young child, but they displayed a similar delight. It was inspiring.

THE REAL SOURCE OF SPIRITUALITY'S BENEFITS

This book opened with some well-researched scholarly claims that belief and religion are good for us. "Believers perform better, have better health, greater happiness and live longer than non-believers."[2] But we were then faced with a conundrum. Was it possible to achieve these benefits, and more, without getting into a box of beliefs and having to sign up to a particular faith or creed?

Throughout this book, then, I have attempted to present the essential concepts, practices, and skills—connect, reflect, and serve; pause, center, watch, and yield—that you will find at the heart of all spiritual approaches and that will deliver those benefits.

But does it really matter whether there are any payoffs and rewards?

The problem with the idea that we shall be rewarded for our effort is that it immediately sets up a concept with which our monkey minds will happily gallop away: that spirituality is to do with a story, a journey that started somewhere and will end somewhere else.

The Hindu prayer that I lovingly quoted in chapter 4 (under "Your Heroic Journey") is a good example of this. The concluding petitions at the ends of the paragraphs are:

> Lead me from ignorance to wisdom.
> Lead me from darkness to light.
> Lead me from death to immortality.

This is all about a journey from one state to another, and our daily spirituality—connect, reflect, and serve—is a way of conducting ourselves on this path, from a closed to an open heart, from a compulsive monkey mind to an expanded consciousness of mindful calm, from a self-centered anxiety to a compassionate generosity toward all things.

FROM! TO! A JOURNEY!

This way of understanding spirituality, that it is a process of development and transformation that occurs as we pass through time, is truthful. But it is also, in its way, a distraction because its focus is on a future goal. Heaven is to come. Our fulfillment lies ahead. But maybe this is all a dream, just another story to fascinate and allure our monkey minds with irresistible promises.

What about right now? What about this moment? Let us forget development, transformation, promises, and the future. There is also the sheer brilliance of just being in the process, here and now.

Let me be less obscure.

If you really love football, then the real magic is in the participation and not in the outcome of the match. If you really love art or movies or books or crafts or work or even lovemaking, then the deepest enjoyment is not to be found in the consummation or final product. The real enjoyment is in being part of it, engaged, embroiled, consumed as it happens.

This too is the real essence of "doing" spirituality and being spiritual. We can focus on all the outcomes—and they are brilliant, the best in the world. But the real payoff, the exhilaration and pure relish and satisfaction, is in the involvement as it happens.

To participate in this grand experience of connection and rapport with the cosmos is, in itself, awesome. To know, here and now, that the essential meaning and purpose of your life is to be found in your heart, compassion, and consciousness is equally awesome. To be dedicated to caring for others, to have an awareness of what other people, plants, and creatures need, and to deliver an affection and nurture and support that relieves their needs, even though you often may forget or be exhausted or selfish—to participate in that process is also unequivocally magnificent.

Just to be involved in spirituality, in life, is the thing. With no head tripping or earnestness about future goals, it is the in-your-face here-and-now experience of spirituality, with its wonder and its struggle, that is supreme.

And then, whatever else is happening in your life, whatever disasters or successes, illnesses or wellness, happiness or unhappiness, you are always enmeshed and participating in this far greater spiritual, soulful, and cosmic reality.

This is what spirituality always gives us—an extra dimension. It is this awareness of an extra dimension and the sheer pleasure of being engaged with it that is, I suggest, the real cause of all the benefits of religion, belief, and spirituality. This extra dimension endows our consciousness, minds, and neuroendocrinologic systems with a stimulation that transcends all the usual physical and psychological stuff. Even when every other part of your life might be a complete loss and disaster, if you are *consciously* part of this cosmic dimension, then you are more *alive* than someone who is glowing with radiant health and success but ignorant of the spiritual context.

I watched a wonderful woman recently battling with an awful cancer that was decimating her body. I shall not describe how horrible it was. But, all the way through it, she was participating in her spiritual life. She was, all the time, present and aware of the spiritual dimension, her opportunity for enlightenment, the wave fields of benevolence. Your monkey mind may want to know whether or not she survived the cancer, and, yes, it healed. But far more important for her was the richness of her spiritual experience.

Whatever condition you are in, spirituality zooms you, enfolds you, unfolds you into this extra dimension. This is not any kind of disassociation, detachment, or transcendence, but an embodied, compassionate, wisdom-building, and thrilling life.

WE ARE STILL ONLY HUMAN

I write this with passion and full engagement, but I also know only too well how we all wrestle with spiritual awareness. Trust no spiritual teacher or expert on human development who tries to make spirituality simple. Sometimes it is simple, but only sometimes. Other times our spiritual growth is a soap opera or Shakespearean drama, triggered either by awful circumstances that are deeply troubling or by events so shallow and meaningless that it is embarrassing to recall them.

During the process of writing this book I had an illness that took me for the first time into an operating theater and under a general anesthetic. With all my decades of disciplined meditation and spiritual practice, preparing for the surgery ought to have been a breeze, but instead it took me a few uncomfortable months to get into the right frame of mind and heart.

I discovered that I had a phobia of general anesthetics, so I used the Inner Smile and visualized myself inside the operating theater and worked with the sensations of panic as they arose in me until I began to feel at ease with the whole procedure.

Naturally my monkey mind needed a happy outcome to the whole story, so I began also to imagine a perfect conclusion. I blessed the surgery team and visualized them working in perfect harmony, fully connected to the wonder and energy of life. I also prayed for any and all help that would make the process graceful and easy.

But, as I did all this inner work, I became haunted by the feeling that something was wrong. Then, slowly, it dawned on me. I realized that my whole approach was, understandably, driven by anxiety, was self-centered, and that I had lost touch with my values. So I came home to the core of what is in this book and its three themes.

- How can I use this situation to **connect** more fully with the wonder and energy of nature and the cosmos?

- How does it help me to **reflect** and grow my compassion and consciousness?

- How can I be of **service** here?

As I came home to these core themes, my feelings and thoughts shifted. Gratitude began to replace anxiety. The real issue was not whether I was ill or well, but whether my consciousness was growing. There was one insight in particular. I could see that I wanted to control the medical team so that they benefited me as much as possible. I was not seeing them as fellow human beings. I was not greeting their souls or supporting their own growth and development, so I began another kind of prayer. It was of blessing, forgiveness, and gratitude:

Whatever happens to me, may my presence and the whole process be a blessing for everyone involved.

I have created and am responsible for this whole situation.

May everyone in the hospital be loved and blessed.

I give thanks for this wonderful situation and lesson.

So why do I really share this story of my surgery with you? In a comradely and companionable way, it is to reassure you. I am old enough and experienced enough to trust my spiritual integrity. My passion is genuine. My spiritual practice is well disciplined and in a deep groove. I am genuinely excited by life and passionately engaged in spirituality. I wake up with it in my awareness. The moment I come to consciousness in my bed every morning, I become mindful and experience my connection. I feel the hum of the wonder and energy all the time. I practice careful and honest self-reflection.

But with all this, when I was ill and anxious, some of my lights dimmed. I was caught in a mood swing, and, even with my years of reflective meditation, I did not immediately recognize that I had been pulled into anxiety and melancholia.

This is human!

So, companion, I seek to comfort you. When you too lose your center and awareness, never despair. We may temporarily get lost—again and again—but it does not matter. We never ever stop participating. Spirituality is not like football or crafts or arts or lovemaking, which are occasional events. In spirituality we are always on the field. Becoming melancholic, being forgetful and disconnected, moody and raging, even venomous—we are never ever excluded from the spiritual dimension.

Just because we are alive, we are perpetually, infinitely, inextricably woven into the spiritual dimension. It is life.

CULTURAL AND SOCIAL CHANGE

We need also to be aware of social engagement. In the twenty-first century we have a cultural opportunity to develop a new approach to spirituality, seeing the essence of all faiths, understanding their high commonality, supporting the new, educated global village of increasing democracy, and integrating the insights of green and psychological development.

The world's great religions are all fourteen hundred years old or older. They have had centuries to develop into their current forms, but they are all deeply colored by their origins. The new spirituality, however, is only just emerging, but without any centralized origin, prophet, or organization. If it continues to reflect modern social realities, then its development will be guided by all the people who are involved in it and instinctively practice it—you and me.

Our inchoate movement, however, requires some common language or else its benefits might never become accessible to mainstream education, health care, and other good agencies of our society. Everyone with the slightest interest in religion or society knows that this new spiritual culture exists. The scholarly statistics are clear that a substantial proportion of the population has moved on from adherence to a single faith and is comfortable with a spirituality that is more general, diverse, and inclusive.

It is time, simply perhaps in the name of just representation, for this new approach to begin to have similar status and voice in all those bodies and areas where the voices of the traditional faiths are heard.

It has good, creative, healthy, and inspiring ideas.

Education

This new approach perfectly understands the connection between spirituality and individual and communal well-being. It is good that children are taught, as they are today, about the world's religions, about citizenship, and about health care. But it would also be good if they were supported in understanding and experiencing that spirituality is about their own personal connection with life's wonder and energy; and that spirituality is dynamic and universal, not dependent upon religions, faiths, and beliefs, but simply intrinsic to being alive.

Health Care

Similarly, when hospitals and other agencies of care assert that spirituality is a crucial aspect of best practice, these assertions can have real contemporary meaning if they communicate about the fuel, healing, and inspiration of connection, and about reflective and self-managed lifelong spiritual development, increasing compassion and consciousness.

Government

When governments, organizations, and businesses, too, claim the high ground and state they have some alignment with spirituality and spiritual values, this too needs to be clear and explicit. How do your policies enable connection with the wonder and energy, support reflective development of the heart and mind, and inspire the highest values and a life of service?

Conflict Resolution

The now-boring debate between secularists and believers around the notion of "God" can also thankfully now be dropped. This new approach to spirituality is not affected by the arguments about whether God exists or not. We have learned to relax into unknowing and yet experience the wonder and benevolence—remaining always present to the suffering and needs of our fellows, in the community of life.

Moreover, the dangerous conflicts between different faiths can be more easily resolved in the context of the new spirituality, which recognizes and celebrates the highest common factors in the world's spiritualities. This simple open-ended question—*in what circumstances do you most easily experience your connection with the wonder and energy of life?*—builds bridges, resolves conflict.

GRAND NARRATIVES AND A MODERN EPIC

Finally, although this book may have illuminated the machinations of our monkey minds and our interpretations, rationalizations, and confabulations, myths can nevertheless be useful. Grand narratives are inspiring. It might be good, therefore, if the new spirituality had a grand narrative that could stand up alongside the stories of Jesus, Mohammed, and Buddha; alongside the Bible, the Koran, the Upanishads, and the Bhagavad Gita.

What might such a grand narrative look like? Just for the enjoyment of it, let me present a possible reverie. It would have to reflect modern realities, the global village, and new circumstances. It would obviously not lead to a single belief, but somehow or another it would support diversity and individualism, community building, and networks of free-flowing information.

It also could not be the story of a single supreme being, prophet, or enlightened one, because today, in our democratized world of opportunity, spiritual experience belongs to all of us. This deep democracy suggests the possibility of a story that is centered on the idea of a collective messiah. Many of the world religions have prophecies that await the return or the arrival of a messiah, an avatar or a prophet, who will deliver humanity and the world to its ultimate destiny: heaven on earth.

Perhaps the grand narrative of the new spirituality could be that together we, as a collective, through the combined energy of our good hearts and mindful compassion, constitute the new messiah. The traditional grand narrative of a single avatar is now democratically dispersed and spread among us all. In unison, we are the avatar.

I know this is an extravagant idea, but one of the blessings of spirituality is surely its infinite extravagance.

Everyone you meet might be the next messiah—but not exclusively. And, provided that we all practice realistic self-reflection and have a sense of humor, never get pompous or earnest, this collective event could be the best party ever.

Why not millions of messiahs? A collective or flock of messiahs? Why not all of us? This surely is a grand theme of spirituality, that we are all part of an evolving and emergent cosmos that is suffused with benevolence; and the destiny for all of us, without exception, is to become fully compassionate and conscious.

In its own way, this idea is not so different from the Christian teaching that Christ is within us all. Indeed the Catholic philosopher and priest Teilhard de Chardin suggested that humanity was destined to function as a "collective Christ."[3]

In this vein too, the Vietnamese Buddhist leader Thich Nhat Hanh, the same teacher whose embrace I found similar to that of a butterfly, once wrote:

The next Buddha will not take the form of an individual.

The next Buddha may take the form of a community;

A community practicing understanding and loving kindness,

A community practicing mindful living. ❧

This may be the most important thing we can do for the survival of the Earth.[4]

It is possible that such a community does already exist, but it is certainly not in a single small geographical location. Perhaps it already exists as a form of collective consciousness if only we could discern it. It might already be found as a network of individuals and groups across the planet, linked by our hearts and our common intention to do good. Perhaps you are part of this.

And, staying in this grand dream, what might be its possible outcome? We might be destined to create heaven on earth. Together, as a collective savior, we achieve a momentum and wave that creates a tipping point for our species and our planet, out of suffering and overwhelming pain, into peace and compassion. And there we would be, caring for each other and all nature's creatures, free and creative, wise and loving.

Of course, all of this is extraordinary, unbelievable, and idealistic, but it is an epic narrative that sings to the tune of the new cultural and social realities—individual spirituality, networked compassionately into the whole community of life.

SPIRITUAL COMPANIONS' GUIDELINES

These guidelines were drawn together after a long consultation process exploring how best to describe the behavior and skills of a spiritual companion—someone who can support others in their spiritual development. My trainings and courses that teach spiritual companionship are centered on them. You are encouraged to add your own guidelines to this list or to rewrite them in a form appropriate for you.

CONNECTION

- Regularly connect with and experience the wonder and energy of existence.

Core Skills

- Can pause, be still at will, and become mindfully present.

- Are centered and grounded.

- Observe what is happening in a kind and good-humored way; witness with compassion.

- Are aware of and yield to the subtle feelings of connection.

Appendix A

REFLECTION

- Self-reflect and manage our behavior, health, and development with compassion, love, and wisdom.

- Are emotionally literate and transparent about our own processes.

- Are in ongoing relationships and groups of peer support, actively seeking and welcoming feedback from others.

- Understand that there are psychological challenges that occur as the everyday self emerges into spiritual consciousness.

- Can take responsibility, apologize, forgive, and receive forgiveness.

- Appreciate that all life is in a continual process of emergence and are comfortable with unknowing.

- Possess an appropriate sense of humor.

SERVICE

- Are aware of and can articulate our values.

- Enable safe and sacred space.

- Provide a nonintrusive, welcoming, healing, and holding presence.

- Listen with care and enable people to clarify and own their own psychospiritual development.

- Can assert clear boundaries and intervene, when appropriate, to stop abuse.

- Celebrate diversity and welcome the fact that there are many different paths of spiritual development.

- Are engaged citizens, actively dedicated to social and ecological health and to honoring the spirit in all beings.

- Are aware of local resources.

- Know our personal and professional limitations and are able to refer appropriately.

For more information go to www.spiritualcompanions.org.

SPIRITUAL EMERGENCY—CARE AND FIRST AID

Sometimes people go through very intense periods of spiritual awakening similar to the one I described in chapter 4, when a young man temporarily went into crisis. In these crises, people find themselves going through such a fast period of personal development that they lose their normal sense of identity and their usual orientation.

In a way, these crises are not dissimilar to sudden grief or trauma, when life's circumstances become so overwhelming that we may be pushed into a period of psychological disorientation. If a loved one dies, for example, it is normal for us to experience a period of unbalance and depression. In fact, we know that such a period is part of the normal process of change, adaptation, and integration. And we also know that if the shock or loss is really great, we may go through a period when it is very difficult to cope with daily affairs. We might have to withdraw from work and social life for a while. This is natural and understandable.

It is the same in intense spiritual awakening. It is natural that occasionally some people may go through a period of disorientation when they cannot handle ordinary life. Their sense of identity is jangled. Their thoughts are perhaps uncontrollable. Their monkey minds are making up many different stories. They also may have strange sensations and feelings in their bodies, similar to electricity or sudden surges of cold or heat.

The problem is this: sometimes the crisis can be so intense that it begins to look and feel like an event that requires psychiatric/medical intervention. It is very helpful, therefore, to have some guidelines for how to distinguish between what is a temporary and healthy process and a disturbance that needs medical care, and also to know some basic first aid.

First of all, it is important to keep in mind that in a "spiritual emergency" people are opening up and changing faster than they can manage. This will have an impact on their nervous systems and the way their minds interpret and explain what is happening. The actual physical experience might elicit the following:

- "There was too much electricity in my brain and head."

- "My chest began to heat up."

- "I could not stop my legs from shaking."

- "It felt like pulses of electricity or energy moving through my body."

In Eastern religious and medical traditions these kinds of sensations are considered to be a normal part of spiritual development. In fact, Ayurvedic medicine (India) and Taoist medicine (China and Japan) have specific anatomical models of how these energies affect the body: the chakra system and the meridians of acupuncture. In particular, attention has been given to what is sometimes called a *kundalini* crisis, the major symptom of which is the sensation of energy or electricity rising from the base of the spine and out through the crown of the head, creating physical and mental agitation.

So be prepared for people to describe the strangest of sensations and to say the weirdest of things to explain their experience. Because of the overstimulation, this experience will usually go hand-in-hand with insomnia and a loss of appetite. Sometimes these symptoms will last only an hour. Sometimes they may go on for a few weeks, even months.

FIRST-AID LIST

When people are inside this kind of crisis here is what they usually find helpful:

- a comforting and nonintrusive presence;
- respect;
- acceptance of their "story";
- encouragement that it is a creative and positive process;
- food;
- rest;
- physical movement;
- touch from safe beings, such as animals and trees;
- stopping of all meditation and psychic exercises because these will amplify the experience;
- withdrawal generally from stimulation;
- someone to attend to practical details such as paying the bills or ringing in to inform an employer of absence.

In the words of Stanislav and Christina Grof, medical practitioners who are very experienced in this field, "The most important task is to give people in crisis a positive context for their experiences and sufficient information about the process that they are going through. It is essential that they move away from the concept of disease and recognize the leading nature of their crisis."[1]

Given a safe space and patience, people will then come out of the crisis in a graceful way and feel stronger and wiser for the experience.

DOES THE CRISIS REQUIRE MEDICAL ATTENTION?

It is important, however, that we be able to discern when a crisis is not a passing and healthy process, but the symptom of something more serious and possibly harmful. In the United States, Dr. David Lukoff is the most experienced researcher in this field, and he suggests a list of indicators that point to the crisis as being positive and manageable.[2] In my own words:

- The individual functioned healthily before the episode.

- There is no history of psychiatric care.

- Intense symptoms last around three months or less.

- There is a clearly definable trigger to the crisis.

- The individual can possess a positive exploratory attitude toward the experience.

- The individual is still able to conceptualize and organize.

- The delusional communications have some mythic coherence (compared, for example, with a general paranoia about a conspiracy).

Online Resources

- www.virtualcs.com: website of Dr. David Lukoff, a very thorough and trustworthy researcher in this field.

- www.spiritualcrisisnetwork.org.uk: website of the United Kingdom Spiritual Crisis Network, who will also be able to advise internationally.

NEXT STEPS AND MORE RESOURCES

NEXT STEPS

In modern spirituality the most important first step is when we decide to take responsibility for our own development. Part of this self-responsibility, then, is to use the wisdom and inspiration of other teachers and teachings to support your enquiry and spiritual practice.

The overall strategy is that, whatever traditions or circumstances you explore, they will always support you in deepening and expanding the three major domains put forward in this book. What we all want is an ongoing and developmental process in which we more consistently, continuously

- connect with the wonder and energy of existence;

- reflect and self-manage the development of our hearts and consciousness; and

- live by our highest values and serve the community of life.

So, whatever the route and scope of your exploration, it is good to keep those three aspects high in your awareness and experience.

In order to support that awareness, I highly recommend that you find some kind of simple daily practice that you can keep to, even if your time is tight and circumstances are difficult. This might just be the daily lighting of a candle and pausing for a few seconds to calm and center or say a prayer or look at the sky or listen to music. There is great power in the ongoing rhythm of simple reminders that are appropriate and suitable for you. You must choose these for yourself.

It is then very useful to find the teachers and circumstances that will help you deepen your spirituality, but where will you find them? Where do you start? Whom can you trust?

SACRED SITES

Well, you can always trust nature, so I want to remind you to notice the natural world and be out in it as much as possible. Visiting sacred sites and places of pilgrimage, too, can be inspiring. You can also trust being calm, silent, and heart-centered.

Online Resources

- www.retreats.org.uk
- www.goingonretreat.com (for Buddhist retreats).

CAREFUL EXPLORATION

If you are new to spirituality, then my advice is that you approach the whole subject carefully, thoughtfully, and patiently, taking the occasional risk in exploring something that is new and unusual for you. Give yourself a couple of years to survey what is available and to get a sense of what interests and inspires you. Do it with the same care and diligence you would give to a new career or to studying for a qualification.

As you explore, you will get a sense of where you would like to dwell longer and deeper. Some people might say that it is absolutely necessary to explore deeply within just one tradition, but, in my opinion, this is not necessarily true at all. Deepening is unique, sovereign, and personal to you. This deepening can happen just as much through exploring diversity as staying in a single path.

TRADITIONAL RELIGIONS AND INTERFAITH

Anyone engaged in spirituality needs to be familiar with the resources and scriptures of the world's great religions. There are literally thousands of books that introduce and describe the world religions. If you are a parent, you will find many books you can read with your children. You can also look at all the textbooks from junior school through to postgraduate studies.

In particular, though, I recommend that you go to the source material: the Bible, the Koran, the Bhagavad Gita, the Tao Te Ching, the Upanishads, and so on. As an online resource I recommend www.sacred-texts.com.

Where possible, visit the places of worship of these traditions and participate in their services.

If you are particularly interested in dialogue between the faiths, then you may want to explore the various interfaith organizations such as the World Parliament of Religions or the Council of Interfaith Communities of the United States.

LECTURES, TRAININGS, WORKSHOPS

It is always valuable to attend lectures, trainings, and workshops. These are good opportunities to taste different approaches. You will need, however, to research what is available in your area. It is worth seeing what is happening in your local further-education or adult-education college. Local libraries usually have notices. So too do whole-food shops and centers for complementary health care.

Appendix C

Some Resources

London: Alternatives Programme of St James's Church, Piccadilly—www.alternatives.org.uk

Birmingham, UK: The Tree of Life Programme—www.treeoflifemagazine.co.uk

Cheltenham, UK: The Isbourne Center—www.isbourne.org

Glastonbury, UK: The Glastonbury Oracle—www.glastonbury-oracle. co.uk

UK: www.holisticmap.org

New York: New York Open Center: www.opencenter.org

San Francisco: California Institute of Integral Studies—www.ciis.edu

Big Sur, CA: Esalen Institute—www.esalen.org

Stockbridge, MA: Kripalu Center for Yoga and Health—www.kripalu.org

New York: Tibet House—www.tibethouse.us

Rhinebeck, NY: Omega Institute for Holistic Studies—http://eomega.org

Notes

Introduction

1. Michael E. McCullough and Brian L. B. Willoughby, "Religion, Self-Regulation, and Self-Control: Associations, Explanations and Implications," *Psychological Bulletin*, January 2009; see also Harold G. Koenig, Michael E. McCullogh, and David B. Larson, *Handbook of Religion and Health* (Oxford: Oxford University Press, 2001).

2. John Button and William Bloom, eds., *The Seekers Guide* (London: HarperCollins, 1989); William Bloom, ed., *The New Age* (London: Rider, 1991); William Bloom, ed., *The Penguin Book of New Age and Holistic Writing* (London: Penguin, 2001); William Bloom, Judy Hall, and David Peters, eds., *The Encyclopedia of Mind Body Spirit: The Complete Guide To Healing Therapies, Esoteric Wisdom* (London: Godsfield, 2010).

3. Ursula King, *The Search for Spirituality: Our Global Quest for Meaning and Fulfilment* (Norwich, UK: Canterbury Press, 2009); Gordon Lynch, *New Spirituality: An Introduction to Belief Beyond Religion* (London: I. B. Tauris, 2007); Paul Heelas, *Spiritualities of Life: New Age Romanticism and Consumptive Capitalism* (Malden, UK: Wiley-Blackwell, 2008).

4. Peter Owen Jones, *Letters from an Extreme Pilgrim: Reflections on Life, Love and the Soul* (London: Rider, 2010).

5. Elizabeth Gilbert, *Eat Pray Love* (London: Bloomsbury, 2007).

6. UNESCO, *Educating for a Sustainable Future: A Transdisciplinary Vision for Concerted Action* (Paris: 1997).

7. "United Nations Declaration of Human Rights," http://www.un.org/en/documents/udhr; "The Earth Charter Initiative," http://www.earthcharterinaction.org/content.

8. Sue Gerhardt, *Why Love Matters: How Affection Shapes a Baby's Brain* (Hove, UK: Routledge, 2004).

231

9. Royal College of Nursing, March 2010, reported in *RCN Bulletin*, no. 250, May 19, 2010.

10. Robert C. Fuller, *Spiritual But Not Religious: Understanding Unchurched America* (New York: Oxford University Press, 2001), 4.

11. Ronald Inglehart and Chris Welzel, *Modernization, Cultural Change and Democracy* (New York: Cambridge University Press, 2005), 48–76.

12. William Johnston, *The Mysticism of "The Cloud of Unknowing"* (New York: Fordham University Press, 2000).

13. Karen Armstrong, *The Case for God: What Religion Really Means* (London: Vintage, 2010).

14. Lynn McTaggart, *The Field* (London: Element Books, 2003); Ervin Laszlo, *Science and the Akashic Field: An Integral Theory of Everything* (Rochester, VT: Inner Traditions, 2007); David Bohm, *Wholeness and the Implicate Order* (London: Routledge Classics, 2002); Fritjof Capra, *Web of Life: A New Synthesis of Mind and Matter* (London: Flamingo, 1997); Adrian B. Smith, *God, Energy and the Field* (Ropley, UK: O Books, 2008).

Chapter 1

1. William James, *The Varieties of Religious Experience* (London: Longman, 1902; London: Penguin Classics, 2004).

2. Brian Thorne, *Infinitely Beloved: The Challenge of Divine Intimacy* (London: Darton, Longman & Todd, 2003) and *Mystical Power of Person Centred Therapy: Hope Beyond Despair* (London: Wiley-Blackwell, 2002).

3. Abraham Maslow, *Religions, Values, and Peak-Experiences* (New York: Viking, 1970); Steve Taylor, *Waking from Sleep* (London: Hay House, 2010).

Chapter 2

1. Edward O. Wilson, *Biophilia* (Cambridge, MA: Harvard University Press, 1984).

2. Candace Pert, *Molecules of Emotion* (London: Simon and Schuster, 1998).

3. William Bloom, *The Endorphin Effect* (London: Piatkus, 2001).

4. Dimitrios Kapogiannis et al., "Cognitive and Neural Foundations of Religious Belief," *Proceedings of theNationalAcademy of Sciences of theUnited States of America* (*PNAS*) 106, no. 12 (March 24, 2009): 4876–81.

5. Andrew Newberg, Eugene G. D'Aquili, and Vince Rowse, *Why God Won't Go Away: Brain Science & the Biology of Belief* (New York: Ballantine Books, 2001).

6. Deepak Chopra, *Perfect Health* (London: Bantam, 2001); Jeff Levin, *God, Faith and Health: Exploring the Spirituality Healing Connection* (New York: John Wiley & Sons, 2002); Gillian White, *Talking About Spirituality in Health Care Practice: A Resource for Health Professionals Working in Multidisciplinary Teams* (London: Jessica Kingsley, 2006); Barbara Ann Brennan, *Hands of Light: Guide to Healing Through the Human Energy Field* (New York: Bantam, 1990); Gill Edwards, *Conscious Medicine: Creating Health and Well-Being in a Conscious Universe* (London: Piatkus, 2010).

7. Neale Donald Walsch, *Conversations with God: An Uncommon Dialogue* (New York: Putnam, 1996).

8. Jon Kabat-Zinn, *Full Catastrophe Living* (London: Piatkus, 2007); Rebecca Crane, *Mindfulness-Based Cognitive Therapy* (London: Routledge, 2008).

9. James George Frazer, *The Golden Bough: A Study in Magic and Religion* (Oxford: Oxford World's Classics, 2009).

10. See note 6 above.

Chapter 3

1. Philip A. Woods, Glenys J. Woods, and Michael Cowie, "'Tears, Laughter, Camaraderie': Professional Development for Head Teachers," *School Leadership & Management* 29, no. 3 (July 2009): 253–75.

2. Jenny Mosley, *Quality Circle Time in the Primary Classroom: Your Essential Guide to Enhancing Self-esteem, Self-discipline and Positive Relationships* (Hyde, UK: LDA, 1998).

3. Eileen Caddy, *Flight into Freedom and Beyond* (Findhorn, UK: Findhorn Press, 2002).

4. Robert Eichinger, "Patterns of Rater Accuracy in 360-degree Feedback," *Perspectives* 27 (2004): 23–25.

5. Henri Nouwen, *Inner Voice of Love* (New York: Image Books, 1999), xvi.

6. M. Amidon, "Groupthink, Politics and the Decision to Attempt the Son Tay Rescue," *Parameters*, US Army War College Quarterly (Autumn 2005): 119–31; David Buchanan and Andrzej Huczynski, *Organisational Behaviour*, 3rd ed. (London: Prentice Hall, 1997); W. Kool, J. T. McGuire, Z. B. Rosen, and M. M. Botvinick, "Decision Making and the Avoidance of Cognitive Demand," *Journal of Experimental Psychology* 139, no. 4 (November 2010): 665-82; Andrei C. Miua, Renata M. Heilmana, and Daniel Houserb, "Anxiety Impairs Decision-Making: Psychophysiological Evidence from an Iowa Gambling Task," *Biological Psychology* 77, no. 3 (March 2008): 353–8.

7. See, for example, Daniel Goleman, *Emotional Intelligence* (London: Bloomsbury, 1996), 11. For techniques on how to conduct this inner dialogue with your feelings, see Ann Weier Cornell, *The Power of Focusing: Finding Your Inner Voice* (Oakland, CA: New Harbinger, 1996), and Hal and Sidra Stone, *Embracing Our Selves: Voice Dialogue Manual* (Novato, CA: Nataraj Publishing, 1989).

8. Stephen Levine, *Healing into Life and Death* (New York: Doubleday, 1987), 127.

9. See, for example, Laura Montgomery, "Illness and Transformation: A Qualitative Study on Self-Perceived Post-traumatic Growth and Spirituality in Women Living with Cancer," paper delivered at the Canadian Society for Social Work and Spirituality, 2008; see http://w3.stu.ca/stu/sites/spirituality/proceedings_2008.html.

10. Margaret Newman, *Health as Expanding Consciousness* (Newbury Park, CA: Sage, 1993).

11. Evelyn Underhill, ed., *The Cloud of Unknowing: The Classic of Medieval Mysticism* (London: Dover, 2003).

Chapter 4

1. Mother Teresa, *Come Be My Light—The Private Writings of the "Saint of Calcutta"* (New York: Doubleday, 2007), pp. 186, 1.

2. Michael Carr, "'Mind-Monkey' Metaphors in Chinese and Japanese Dictionaries," *International Journal of Lexicography* 6, no. 3 (1993): 149–80.

3. Iain McGilchrist, *The Master and His Emissary, The Divided Brain and the Making of the Western World* (New Haven: Yale University Press, 2009), 81; see also, for example, Ronald Kotulak, *Inside the Brain: Revolutionary Discoveries of How the Mind Works*, rev. ed. (Kansas City: Andrews McMeel Publishing, 1997).

4. *Diagnostic and Statistical Manual of Mental Disorders* (Arlington: American Psychiatric Publishing, 2000), 62.89: 685.

5. Roger J. Woolger, *Other Lives, Other Selves: A Jungian Psychotherapist Discovers Past Lives* (London: Thorsons, 1999); Brian L. Weiss, *Many Lives, Many Masters: The True Story of a Prominent Psychiatrist, His Young Patient and the Past-life Therapy That Changed Both Their Lives* (London: Piatkus 1994).

6. Daniel Smith, *Muses, Madmen and Prophets—Hearing Voices and the Borders of Sanity* (New York: Penguin, 2008).

7. Wing-Tsit Chan, *Chinese Philosophy* (Princeton: Princeton University Press, 1969), 481.

8. John Michell, *How the World is Made* (London: Thames and Hudson, 2009), 2. For an in-depth examination of these dynamics, see Pascal Boyer, *Religion Explained: The Human Instincts that Fashion Gods, Spirits and Ancestors* (New York: Vintage Books, 2002).

9. José Saramago, *The Double* (Orlando: Vintage Books, 2004), 228.

10. Alain de Botton, *Status Anxiety* (London: Hamish Hamilton, 2004).

Chapter 5

1. Eckhart Tolle, *A New Earth: Create a Better Life* (London: Penguin, 2009).

2. Chesley Sullenberger, *My Highest Duty: My Search for What Really Matters* (New York: William Morrow, 2009); William Prochnau, *Miracle on the Hudson: The Extraordinary Real-Life Story Behind Flight 1549, by the Survivors* (New York: Ballantine Books, 2010).

3. Allan Luks, *The Healing Power of Doing Good: The Health and Spiritual Benefits of Helping Others* (New York: Fawcett Books, 1992); David Hamilton, *Why Kindness is Good for You* (London: Hay House, 2010).

4. Elizabeth W. Dunn et al., "On the Costs of Self-interested Economic Behavior: How Does Stinginess Get Under the Skin?" *Journal of Health and Psychology* 15, no. 4 (May 11, 2010): 627-33.

5. Luks, *Healing Power of Doing Good*; Hamilton, *Why Kindness is Good for You.*

6. Horace E. Dobbs, *Dolphin Healing: The Science and Magic of Dolphins* (London: Piatkus, 2000); Rachel Smolker, *To Touch a Wild Dolphin: A Journey of Discovery with the Sea's Most Intelligent Creatures* (New York: Anchor Books, 2002).

7. Quoted by Sara Lippincott, *Los Angeles Times*, September 20, 2009, http://www.latimes.com/entertainment/news/la-ca-frans-de-waal20-2009sep20,0,2921618.story. See Frans de Waal, *The Age of Empathy* (New York: Random House, 2009).

8. Edward O. Wilson, *Biophilia* (Cambridge, MA: Harvard University Press, 1984).

9. Sue Gerhardt, *Why Love Matters: How Affection Shapes a Baby's Brain* (London: Routledge, 2004); Louis Cozolino, *The Neuroscience of Human Relationships: Attachment and the Developing Social Brain* (New York: Norton, 2006).

10. James H. Fowler and Nicholas A. Christakis, "Dynamic Spread of Happiness in a Large Social Network: Longitudinal Analysis over 20 Years in the Framingham Heart Study," *British Medical Journal* (December 4, 2008): 337:a2338.

11. Helena Norberg-Hodge, *Ancient Futures: Learning from Ladakh* (London: Rider, 2000); Carol Graham, *Happiness Around the World: The Paradox of Happy Peasants and Miserable Millionaires* (Oxford: Oxford University Press, 2009).

12. Carl Rogers, *On Becoming a Person* (London: Constable, 2004).

13. See, for example, St. Benedict, *The Rule of St. Benedict* (Collegeville, MN: Liturgical Press, 1968) and Thich Nhat Hanh, *Stepping into Freedom: Rules of Monastic Practice for Novices* (Berkeley, CA: Parallax Press, 1997).

14. Dale Carnegie, *How to Stop Worrying and Start Living* (New York: Pocket, 1990).

Chapter 6

1. Ervin Lazlo, *Akashic Experience: Science and the Cosmic Memory Field* (Rochester, VT: Inner Traditions, 2009).
2. William Walker Atkinson, *The Secret Doctrine of the Rosicrucians* (New York: Cosimo, 2010); Manly P. Hall, *Secret Teachings of All Ages* (New York: Jeremy P. Tarcher, 2004).
3. Barbara Ann Brennan, *Hands of Light: Guide to Healing Through the Human Energy Field* (New York: Bantam, 1990); Pamela Miles, *Reiki: A Comprehensive Guide* (New York: Jeremy P. Tarcher, 2008).
4. Christoph Riedweg, *Pythagoras: His Life, Teaching, and Influence* (Ithaca, NY: Cornell University Press, 2005).
5. William Johnston, *Silent Music: The Science of Meditation* (New York: Fordham University Press, 1997).
6. Gerda Boyesen, "How I Developed Biodynamic Psychotherapy," in *About a Body*, ed. Jenny Corrigall, Helen Payne, and Heward Wilkinson (London: Routledge, 2006), 135.
7. See, for example, Pierre Pradervand, *The Gentle Art of Blessing* (Llandeilo, UK: Cygnus, 2010).
8. Dalai Lama and Renuka Singh, *The Path to Tranquility: Daily Wisdom* (New York: Penguin, 2002).
9. Victoria E. Shook, *Ho'oponopono: Contemporary Uses of a Hawaiian Problem Solving Process* (Honolulu: University of Hawaii Press, 1986); Joe Vitale and Hew Len, *Zero Limits* (Hoboken, New Jersey: Wiley, 2007).

Conclusion

1. David Hay and Rebecca Nye, *The Spirit of the Child* (London: Jessica Kingsley Publishers, 1998), 94–95.
2. Michael E. McCullough and Brian L. B. Willoughby, "Religion, Self-Regulation, and Self-Control: Associations, Explanations and Implications," *Psychological Bulletin* (January 2009).
3. Pierre Teilhard de Chardin, *The Phenomenon of Man* (New York: Harper, 1976).

4. Thich Nhat Hanh, "The Next Buddha May Be A Sangha," *Inquiring Mind* 10, no. 2 (Spring 1994).

Appendix B

1. Stanislav Grof and Christina Grof, eds., *Spiritual Emergency: When Personal Transformation Becomes A Crisis* (New York: Warner Books, 1989), 195.
2. David Lukoff, "The Diagnosis of Mystical Experiences with Psychotic Features," *Journal of Transpersonal Psychology* 17, no. 2 (1985): 155-81.

Glossary

centered: earthed (q.v.), mindful (q.v.), and benevolent all at the same time.

consciousness: your general ability to be aware of what is happening in and around you. There is an important paradox or predicament here: sometimes you will be self-conscious, awake to, and self-aware of your ability to be conscious, and sometimes you will not be self-conscious and awake, but just on automatic pilot.

developmental psychology: the scientific study of psychological changes during the course of the lifespan.

earthed: fully embedded in your physical body and aware of your physicality; the opposite of being spaced out. Synonymous with grounded (q.v.) and similar to *hara* (q.v.).

empathic awareness: the ability to sense and feel atmospheres and moods in people and places.

grounded: fully embedded in your physical body and aware of your physicality; the opposite of being spaced out. Synonymous with earthed (q.v.) and similar to *hara* (q.v.).

hara: a Japanese word used in the Samurai and martial-arts traditions, denoting that someone has a stable, strong, chivalrous, and dignified presence. This is brought about by having your physical center of gravity seated in the area of the lower abdomen and having a full sense of your physical body, which then acts as a physical anchor for a general state of compassion and mindfulness.

holistic: recognizing that all things are connected, interdependent, and part of a greater whole.

holistic approach to spirituality: an openhearted and open-minded approach, honoring the essence of all spiritual traditions.

metaphysics: the study of subtle energies and invisible dimensions.

mindfulness: the ability to take a mental pause and observe, in a detached and philosophical fashion, what you are doing and feeling and what is going on around you. Historically it has been one of the key elements of meditation and is currently being developed in the UK's National Health Service as an adjunct to cognitive behavioral therapy to support mental health.

mystic: someone who has had a spiritual experience and felt a connection with the wonder and energy of creation and then decided that exploring and deepening that experience is the most important focus of his or her life.

neurotheology: the study of brain activity and its connection with the subjective experiences we would call spiritual; sometimes called *spiritual neuroscience* or *biotheology.*

numinous: describing a sense of being close to divinity and wonder.

psychoneuroimmunology (PNI): the study of the interconnectedness between the nervous and immune systems and our psychological processes.

religion: an organized set of beliefs and customs.

rimpoche (also spelled rinpoche): an honorific title of a highly regarded teacher in Tibetan Buddhism.

shamanism: the ability to talk with the spirits of the natural world and see into the world beyond death.

soul: the core aspect of one's psychology and consciousness that is always connected to the wonder and energy of all life.

spirituality: the individual and personal experience of the wonder and energy of nature and the cosmos.

Tao: in Chinese philosophy, the absolute principle, signifying the "way" that is in harmony with the natural order.

Recommended Reading

General Modern Texts

Anand, Margo. *The New Art of Sexual Ecstasy: Following the Path of Sacred Sexuality*. London: Thorsons, 1990.

Bloom, William. *First Steps: An Introduction to Spiritual Practice*. Findhorn, Scotland: Findhorn Press, 1993.

———. *Soulution: The Holistic Manifesto*. London: Hay House, 2005.

Cameron, Julia. *The Artist's Way*. New York: Pan, 1995.

Campbell, Joseph. *The Masks of God: Primitive Mythology*. New York: Penguin Books, 1976.

Castaneda, Carlos. *The Teachings of Don Juan: A Yaqui Way of Knowledge*. London: 2004.

Dawes, Joycelin, Janice Dolley, and Ike Isaksen. *The Quest: Exploring a Sense of Soul*. Alresford, UK: O Books, 2005.

Edwards, Gill. *Living Magically*. London: Piatkus, 1999.

Harner, Michael. *The Way of the Shaman*. San Francisco: Harper, 1992.

Hennezel, Marie de. *The Warmth of Your Heart Prevents Your Body from Rusting*. London: Rodale, 2011.

Hillman, James. *The Soul's Code*. New York: Bantam, 1997.

Iyengar, B. K. S. *Light on Yoga*. London: Thorsons, 2001.

Lovelock, J. E. *Gaia—A New Look at Life on Earth*. Oxford: Oxford University Press, 2000.

Macy, Joanna. *World as Lover, World as Self*. Berkeley: Parallax, 2007.

Michell, John. *The New View Over Atlantis*. London: Thames and Hudson, 1983.

Myss, Caroline. *Anatomy of Spirit*. New York: Bantam, 1997.

Recommended Reading

O'Donohue, John. *Anam Cara—Spiritual Wisdom from the Celtic World*. New York: Bantam, 1999.

Seed, John, Joanna Macy, and Pat Fleming. *Thinking Like a Mountain: Towards a Council of All Beings*. Gabriola Island, Canada: New Catalyst Books, 2007.

Shucman, Helen. *A Course in Miracles*. Mill Valley, CA: Foundation for Inner Peace, 1996.

Sogyal Rinpoche. *The Tibetan Book of Living and Dying*. London: Rider, 2002.

Spangler, David. *Everyday Miracles: The Inner Art of Manifestation*. New York: Bantam, 1998.

Starhawk. *The Spiral Dance: A Rebirth of the Ancient Religions of the Great Goddess*. New York: Harper, 1999.

Tolle, Eckhart. *The Power of Now*. New York: New World, 2004.

Walsch, Neale Donald. *Conversations with God*. London: Hodder, 1999.

Williamson. Marianne. *Return to Love*. New York: HarperCollins, 1996.

Yoganada, Paramahansa. *Autobiography of a Yogi*. Los Angeles: Indy-publish, 2004.

Sacred Sites

Olsen, Brad. *Sacred Places North America: 108 Destinations*. San Francisco: CCC Publishing, 2008.

Meehan, Cary. *The Traveller's Guide to Sacred Ireland*. Glastonbury: Gothic Image, 2002.

Michell, John. *The Traveller's Guide to Sacred England*. Glastonbury: Gothic Image, 2003.

Whiteaker, Stafford. *The Good Retreat Guide*. London: Hay House, 2010.

Recommended Reading

Scholarly Overview

Heelas, Paul, Linda Woodhead, Benjamin Seel, and Bronislaw Szerszynski. *The Spiritual Revolution: Why Religion Is Giving Way to Spirituality*. Oxford: Wiley-Blackwell, 2004.

King, Ursula. *The Search for Spirituality: Our Global Quest for Meaning and Fulfillment*. Norwich, UK: Canterbury Press, 2009.

Lynch, Gordon. *New Spirituality: An Introduction to Belief Beyond Religion*. London: I. B. Tauris, 2007.

Tacey, David. *The Spirituality Revolution: The Emergence of Contemporary Spirituality*. London: Routledge, 2004.

Science and Spirituality

Bohm, David. *Wholeness and the Implicate Order*. London: Routledge, 2002.

Capra, Fritjof. *The Tao of Physics*. London: Flamingo, 1992.

Davies, Paul. *God and the New Physics*. London: Penguin, 2006.

Sheldrake, Rupert. *A New Science of Life*. London: Paladin, 1983.

Zukav, Gary. *The Dancing Wu Li Masters: An Overview of the New Physics*. New York: Harper, 2001.

Spiritual Emergency—Care and First Aid

Bloom, William. *Feeling Safe*. London: Piatkus, 2008.

———. *Psychic Protection*. London: Piatkus, 2010.

Bragdon, Emma. *The Call of Spiritual Emergency: From Personal Crisis to Personal Transformation*. New York: Harper, 1990.

———. *Sourcebook for Helping People in Spiritual Emergency*. Woodstock, VT: Lightening Up Press, 1994.

Clarke, Isabel, ed. *Psychosis and Spirituality*. Chichester, UK: Wiley-Blackwell, 2010.

Recommended Reading

Griffith, James, and Melissa Elliot Griffith. *Encountering the Sacred in Psychotherapy: How to Talk with People About Their Spiritual Lives*. New York: Guilford Press, 2001.

Grof, Stanislav. *The Stormy Search for the Self: A Guide to Personal Growth through Transformative Crisis*. New York: Jeremy P. Tarcher, 1997.

Grof, Stanislav, and Christina Grof, eds. *Spiritual Emergency: When Personal Transformation Becomes A Crisis*. New York: Warner Books, 1989.

Jung, Carl. *The Archetypes and the Collective Unconscious*. London: Routledge, 1991.

Nelson, John E. *Healing the Split—Integrating Spirit into Our Understanding of the Mentally Ill*. Albany, NY: State University of New York Press, 1994.

Rowan, John. *Subpersonalities: The People Inside Us*. London: Routledge, 1989.

Smith, Daniel B. *Muses, Madmen and Prophets—Hearing Voices and the Borders of Sanity*. New York: Penguin, 2008.

Spiritual Health and Healing

Angelo, Jack. *The Spiritual Healing Handbook: How to Develop Your Healing Powers and Increase Your Spiritual Awareness*. London: Piatkus, 2007.

Bailey, Alice. *Esoteric Healing*. London: Lucis Press, 2001.

Brennan, Barbara Ann. *Hands of Light: Guide to Healing Through the Human Energy Field*. New York: Bantam, 1990.

Chopra, Deepak. *Ageless Body, Timeless Mind*. New York: Rider, 1993.

Gaskin, Ina May. *Spiritual Midwifery*. Summertown, TN: Book Publishing Co., 1980.

Gerber, Richard. *Vibrational Medicine*. Rochester, VT: Bear, 1996.

Wilber, Ken, and Terry Patten. *Integral Life Practice: A 21st-Century Blueprint for Physical Health, Emotional Balance, Mental Clarity, and Spiritual Awakening*. Boston: Integral Books, 2008.

Spiritual Psychology

Ferrucci, Piero. *What We May Be: Techniques for Psychological and Spiritual Growth through Psychosynthesis.* New York: Jeremy P. Tarcher, 2009.

Gilbert, Paul. *The Compassionate Mind.* London: Constable, 2010.

Jung, Carl. *Memories, Dream, Reflections.* New York: Vintage Books, 1989.

Kübler-Ross, Elisabeth. *On Death and Dying.* London: Routledge, 1973.

Moore, Thomas. *Care of the Soul.* London: Piatkus, 1992.

Peck, M. Scott. *The Road Less Traveled: A New Psychology of Love, Traditional Values and Spiritual Growth.* New York: Rider, 2003.

Rowan, John. *The Transpersonal: Spirituality in Psychotherapy and Counselling.* London: Routledge, 2005.

Weiss, Brian. *Many Lives, Many Masters.* London: Piatkus, 1994.

Woolger, Roger. *Other Lives, Other Selves.* New York: Doubleday, 1999.

Index

A

Abhinavagupta, 66
acupuncture meridians, 224
addiction, 136, 144
affection, 170–72
Alister Hardy Religious Experience
    Research Centre, 35
aliveness, 67
Allah, 29
Alternatives Programme, 18
American Psychiatric Association
    (APA), 132
animals, empathy of, 169–70
apology, 202–3
architecture, sacred, 65
Armstrong, Karen, 28
asceticism, 91
Atisha Dipankara Shrijnana, 198
attachment, 134–36
Augean stables, 120
aura, 23
avatar, 216
awakening
    dissatisfaction and, 90–93
    intense or sudden, 125–28,
        223–26
    triggers to, 91
Ayurvedic medicine, 224

B

BBC Radio 4, 11
behavioral psychology, 137
belief(s)
    as beneficial, 208
    hiding, 24–26
    research into, 1
    style, tone, and language of,
        47–48
benevolent field, 73, 197, 202
Bernard of Clairvaux, Saint, 177
Bhagavad Gita, 216, 229
Bible, 216, 229
Big Bang, 62, 140
biodynamic psychotherapy, 187–89
biophilia (love of nature), 62
biotheology, 63
blessing, 192
Bloom, William
    experiences of, 25–27, 56–61, 88,
        92–93, 103–5
    life of, 8–12
    values of, 19
Bohm, David, 30
bottom, 70, 186
Boyesen, Gerda, 187–89
brain, 63, 131
Brhadaranyaka Upanishad, 122

British Medical Journal, 171
Buddha, 74–75, 216–17
Buddha consciousness, 29
Buddhism
    asceticism in, 91
    Inner Smile in, 73–74
    monkey mind in, 130
    negativity and, 197–98
    service in, 160–61, 186
    spiritual development in, 121
    suffering and, 152–53
burnout, 176–77

C
Caddy, Eileen, 95, 100–2
calmness, 185, 189
Campbell, Joseph, 122
Capra, Fritjof, 30, 126
caring, 170–72
Carnegie, Dale, 178
Case for God, The (Armstrong),
    28
centering
    as core skill, 56, 63, 70–72
    in Eucharist, 59
    kind watchfulness and, 6–8
    in self-reflection, 103
center of gravity, 70
ceremony, 183
chakra system, 224
change, cultural and social, 213–16
chi (energy), 182
children
    centering and mindfulness in,
        195–96

    spirituality of, 207
    wonder in, 207
chivalry, 165–67, 186, 202
Christakis, Nicholas A., 171
Christianity
    asceticism in, 91
    "emptying" in mystical, 116
    energy field and, 183
    greeting Christ within, 174
    healing work in, 193–94
    imperfect humanity in, 121
    love in, 29
    negativity and, 198
    service in, 160–61, 186
    unworthiness in, 46
Circle Time, 95
citizenship, 21
Cloud of Unknowing, The
    (anonymous), 28, 116
"collective Christ," 217
collective consciousness, 217–18
*Come Be My Light - The Private
    Writings of the "Saint of
    Calcutta"* (Mother Teresa), 128
compassion, 204–5
conditioning, 137
confidence, 83
conflict resolution, 215
congruence, 174
connection
    aspects of, 43
    with energy and wonder, 5–6,
        20, 27, 33–34, 212
    gateways to, 37–38
    guidelines for, 219

as key spiritual practice, 5–6
reclaiming, 207–8
as spiritual experience, 33–34
consciousness
    altered by music, 53
    as inner deity, 75
    of one brain cell, 155
containment, 140–43
Conversations with God (Walsch), 64
core skills. *See also* centering; pausing; watching; yielding
    centering as, 70–72
    of good team leaders, 189
    guidelines for, 219
    as means of spiritual connection, 55–56, 63–64
    pausing, 64–69
    in self-reflection, 101–6
    watching, 72–75
    yielding, 76–78
cosmos
    as benevolent, 29
    as context, 200
Council of Interfaith Communities, 229
courage, 165–67
cravings, 136
creation, 29
Cretan bull, 120–21
crisis
    awakening from, 154
    as opportunity, 112
    spiritual, 127, 223–26
culture, changing, 14–16

D
Dancing Wu Li Masters, The (Zukav), 126
deity, as Father and Mother, 140
democracy, 216
desire, 152–53
detachment, 149–51
developmental psychology, 22
de Waal, Frans, 170
Diagnostic and Statistical Manual of Mental Disorders (APA), 132–33
discipline, 45–46
dissatisfaction, 90, 112
distant healing, 193–94
diversity, 15–17
doctrine, 45
doing good. *See* service
dolphins, 169
duration
    of connection experience, 43
    as technique, 54
"duvet spirituality," 81–84

E
Earth Charter, 19, 20
Eat, Pray, Love (Gilbert), 14
Eckhart, Meister, 78
education
    changing methods of, 15
    spirituality in, 24, 214–15
electromagnetism, 23
elitism
    connection and, 44–45
    in style tone, and language, 47–48

Index

emergence, 127

emergency, spiritual, 127, 223–26

emotional literacy/intelligence, 110

emotions, 63–64

empathy, 169–70, 174

emptying, 115–16

endorphins, 63

energy and energy field
  as interconnected system,
    197–98
  names for, 182–83
  as natural vitality, 84, 182–83
  overwhelming, 128
  in spiritual connection, 3, 5–6,
    27, 49, 62, 80, 84, 181–82

England and Wales Education Act
  of 2002, 24

enlightenment, 93

environment, values and, 20

esoteric schools, 183

ethics
  religions and, 18–19, 161
  statements of, 19–21

Eucharist, 57–58

exercises
  apology and forgiveness, 203–4
  beliefs and unknowing, 146–47
  breathe in negativity, breathe out
    blessing, 198–200
  bridge-building conversation,
    50
  circumstances for connection,
    55
  clarify your values, 163–64
  duvet spirituality, 82–84

embodiment and centering,
  71–72

gratitude and awakening, 112–13

greeting someone's soul, 174–75

holding the situation, 190–91

Inner Smile, 75–76

introducing reflection, 94

mindfulness, 68–69

natural meditation, 106–8

noticing connection, 37

oases of nourishment, 116–17

planning spiritual practice, 81

psychology of resistance,
  139–40

recalling moment of connection,
  44

recalling previous 24 hours,
  99–100

remembering and appreciating,
  61

self-healing meditation, 110–12

sending healing to others,
  194–95

spiritual styles, 40

story of your life, 148–49

what do we really need, 151–52

yielding to experience, 78–79

your family of nature and
  cosmos, 179–80

expansion, 144

experience
  nature and depth of, 42–44
  varieties of religious, 33–37

Extreme Pilgrim (television
  program), 14

F

fasting, 91

feedback, 101

feelings, 64, 76

Field, The (McTaggert), 30

Findhorn Foundation, 96

first-aid list for spiritual crises, 225

forgiveness, 200–3

Foundation for Holistic Spirituality, 25

Fowler, James H., 171

Francis of Assisi, Saint, 204

Frazer, James George, 74

Freud, Sigmund, 138

friends, 80

Fuller, Robert, 25

G

generosity, 167–68

geometry, sacred, 65

Gilbert, Elizabeth, 14

giving, 204

Glastonbury, 192

global village, 13–15

God

    concept of, 27–29

    debates over, 215

    "God spot" and, 63

    Mother Teresa and, 128

    mythology of, 145

    priestly relationship with, 45

God, Energy and the Field (Smith), 30

goddesses, 74–75

Golden Bough, The (Frazer), 74

good humor, as service, 185

good people, 185–87

goodwill, 73, 115

government, 215

gratitude, 60–61

green movement, 22

greeting the Christ within, 174

Grof, Stanislav and Christina, 225

grounding. *See also* centering

    as core skill, 56, 70–72

    in Eucharist, 59

    in self-reflection, 103

guidelines of Spiritual Companions, 11, 219–21

H

hajj (pilgrimage), 135

hara (centering), 70, 186

Harvard Business School, 20

Hay, David, 207

healing

    distant, 193–94

    Polynesian, 202

    prayer in, 192–93

Healing Into Life and Death (Levine), 114

Health as Expanding Consciousness (Newman), 114–15

health care, 64, 215

hearing voices, 133–34

heaven, 207

Hercules, 120–21

hero's journey, 120–23

Hew Len, Dr. Ihaleakala, 202

hierarchies, religions and, 45

Index

Hinduism
    asceticism in, 91
    Namaste in, 174
    Nirvana in, 29
    spiritual development in, 121
    unworthiness and karma in, 46
"holding" a situation, 189–90
Holy Spirit/Ghost, 30
homeostasis, 138–39
honesty, 97, 175–76
Ho'oponopono Prayer of Apology,
    202
hormones, 63
*How to Win Friends and Influence
    People* (Carnegie), 178
Huddleston, Trevor, 17–18
humanity as "collective Christ," 217
humility, 175–76
Hydra, 120

I

identity, 147–48
illness
    as opportunity, 112
    spiritual, 123–25
inclusion, in values statement, 20
information, 13–14, 115
Inner Smile
    in exercises, 107, 110, 112, 139,
        163, 187, 190, 194–95
    as kind attention to self, 73–74,
        103
    as self-forgiveness, 201
    in spiritual practice, 77, 82, 154,
        172

inner worlds, 74–75
Inquisition, 183
inspiration, 176–77
interfaith organizations, 229
introspection, 103
irritation, 110
Islam
    asceticism in, 91
    connection in, 49–50
    energy field and, 183
    imperfect humanity and, 121
    unworthiness in, 46
isolation, 91

J

James, William, 35, 46
Jesus, 75, 80, 168, 198, 216
Johnston, William, 28, 187
Jones, Peter Owen, 13
journals, 98
Judaism
    connection in, 48–49
    energy field and, 183
    imperfect humanity in, 121
    service in, 160–61
    tree of life in, 74
    unworthiness in, 46

K

Kabbala, 74
karma, 46
kindness to self, 72–75, 103–4, 201
Knights Templar, 183
Koran, 216, 229
kundalini, 224

Index

L

language, 47–48
Laszlo, Ervin, 30
leaders, 189
Levine, Stephen, 114
Lord's Prayer, 193, 201
lotus, 121
love, 29, 200
Lukoff, David, 226

M

magic of life, 84, 207
martial arts, 70, 182, 184, 186
martyrdom, 147–48
material world, 183
McCullough, Michael E., 1
McGilchrist, Iain, 132
McTaggert, Lynn, 30
meaningfulness, of connection, 43
Mecca, 135
media, 15
medicine, self-management in, 15
medicine men, 123, 181–82
meditation, 104–8, 110–12
messiah, 216–17
metaphors
    "duvet spirituality" as, 82
    Hercules as, 120–21
    for visualization, 74
Milarepa, 6
mindfulness. *See also* pausing
    in children, 195–96
    as core skill, 56, 63–69, 102
    in Eucharist, 59
Mitchell, John, 145

Mohammed, 216
monkey mind, 130–33, 144–45
Monty Python's Life of Brian (film),
    122
moods
    affecting world, 183, 184
    choosing, 74
    kind watchfulness and, 72, 144
morality, 18–19, 160–61
multisource assessment, 98
music, 53, 79
mysteries, 183
*Mysticism of "The Cloud of
    Unknowing"* (Johnston), 28
myths, 144–46

N

Namaste, 174
narratives, grand, 216–18
National Federation of Spiritual
    Healers, 20
National Health Service, 24
nature
    caring for, 177–78
    gratitude and, 60–61
    resistance as force of, 140–42
    sociobiology and, 62
    in spiritual experience, 54
negativity, transforming, 197–98
nervous system, 138
neuroendocrinologic system, 74
neuroendocrinologic state (mood),
    72
neuroscience, 63, 138
neurotheology, 62–63

neurotransmitters, 63
Newman, Margaret, 114–15
new spirituality. *See also* spirituality
    democracy and, 182, 216
    grand narrative of, 216–18
    as movement, 12–13, 214
    next steps in, 227–29
    values of, 17–18, 24, 159–62
New Year resolutions, 136, 137
Nirvana, 29
Noble Eightfold Path, 160
nourishment, 116–17
Nouwen, Henri, 98
Nye, Rebecca, 207

O

observation. *See also* watching
    as core skill, 56, 72–75
    in Eucharist, 59
    in self-reflection, 103–4
Olslo Conference on Freedom of
    Belief (1998), 10–11
one-brain-cell approach, 153–55,
    172
Open Mystery School, 11
original sin, 46, 121
others, seeing best in, 173

P

paganism, 28
pain, 112
pausing. *See also* mindfulness
    as core skill, 64–69
    difficulty in, 66–68
    in self-reflection, 102

Pavlov's dog, 137
peak experiences, 46–47,
    128–29
Peale, Norman Vincent, 97
Pert, Candace, 63
pilgrimage, 135
Plato, 95
Pogacnik, Marco, 178
polarity, 140–42
Polynesian healing, 202
pots, 74
practices, three key spiritual, 4–6
prana (energy), 84, 182
prayers
    of blessing, 212–13
    of forgiveness, 202, 212–13
    of gratitude, 78, 212–13
    in healing, 192–93
    Hindu, 122, 209
    Ho'oponopono Prayer of
        Apology, 202
    Lord's Prayer, 193, 201
    reflective, 96
    for spiritual path, 122
presence
    affecting those around us, 181
    kind and mindful, 187–89
    in psychotherapy, 188
priests
    creating vibration, 181–82
    as disconnected, 56–58
prophecies, 216
Psychological Bulletin, 1
psychology
    behavioral, 137

psychoanalytic school of, 138
spiritual, 142–44
psychoneuroimmunology (PNI),
62–63
purification, 45
Pythogorean school, 184

Q
qi (energy), 84, 182
qi gung, 70, 78
quantum field, 30

R
rationalization, 132
reflection
elements of, 89–92
examples of, 95–98
guidelines for, 220
as key spiritual practice, 5–6,
212
for self-healing, 108–10
reiki, 184
relationships, 21, 170–72
relaxation. *See also* centering
as core skill, 56, 70–72
in Eucharist, 59
in self-reflection, 103
"Religion, Self-Regulation, and
Self-Control" (McCullough and
Willoughby), 1
religions
as beneficial, 208
comforting myths of, 146
ethical teachings in, 161
moral guidance of, 160–61

resources of, 229
style, tone, and language of,
47–48
teachings of, 13
varieties of experience in,
34–35
repetition, 54, 91–92
repression, 138
research, on belief, 1
resistance to change, 120, 134–39,
140–42
respect
values statement and, 20
responsibility
for mood and vibrations, 23
values statement and, 21
retreats, 83
ritual, 183
Rogers, Carl, 173–74
Rosicrucians, 183
Rumi, 77–78

S
sacred architecture, 65
sacred geometry, 65
sacred mechanics, 183
sacred sites, 228
sacred texts, 229
Samurai, 186
Saramago, José, 145–46
satsang (spiritual gatherings), 80
science, of spiritual experience,
62–63
Science and the Akashic Field
(Laszlo), 30

self
　　detachment from story, 149–51
　　sense of, 147–48
self-acceptance, 201
self-auditing, 89
self-delusion, 98
self-determination and diversity,
　　15–17
self-esteem, 83
self-forgiveness, 201
self-gratification, 167
self-healing, 108–12
selfishness, 167
self-management, 93, 143, 155
self-reflection. *See* reflection
self-responsibility
　　for mood and vibrations, 23
　　values statement and, 21
self-sacrifice, 45
sensations, 34, 76
separation of church and state,
　　16
Sermon on the Mount, 160
service
　　good humor as, 185
　　guidelines for, 220–21
　　healing prayer as, 192–93
　　as key spiritual practice, 5–6,
　　　212
　　mood and vibration in, 184
　　religions and, 160–61
　　as way of connecting, 167–70
Shao Yong, 140
Shekinah (glory of divine presence),
　　29

Sikhism, 121
silence, 54
Silent Music (Johnston), 187
skills, core. *See* core skills
Smith, Adrian B., 30
Smith, Daniel, 134
"social wealth," 171
society
　　changing, 15–16
　　moods and attitudes in, 171
sociobiology, 62, 170
soul, greeting someone's, 174
Southwark College, 92
speaking in tongues, 128
Spirit of the Child (Hay and Nye),
　　207
Spiritual But Not Religious (Fuller),
　　25
Spiritual Companions, 11, 150
　　guidelines of, 219–21
spiritual connection. *See also*
　　connection
　　experience of, 63–64
　　wonder and energy in, 3, 5, 27,
　　　49, 62, 80, 181–82
spiritual development, 82
　　next steps in, 227–29
　　paradox and poignancy of,
　　　88–89
　　vision of, 87
spiritual illness and healing, 123–25,
　　184
spirituality. *See also* new spirituality
　　benefits of, 2–4
　　depth of, 51–52

as independent of external life,
82–83
source of benefits in, 208–9
style, tone, and language in,
47–48
styles of, 38–40
talking about, 26–27
values statement and, 20–21
spiritual path, 120–23, 209–11,
228–29
spiritual practices and experiences
elitism and, 44–48
extending to natural world,
177–78
as ongoing, 40–42
planning, 79–80
repetition and duration in, 54
science of, 62–63
St. James's Church, 17, 172, 186
stagnation, 91
stress, 167
style, of connection experience, 43
suffering, 152–53
Sufism, 186
Sullenberger, Chesley, 165–66
surrendering. *See* yielding
symbols, 74, 121
Symeon the Stylite, Saint, 6

T
tai chi, 70, 182
tantra, Inner Smile in, 73–74
Taoism
Inner Smile in, 73–74
monkey mind in, 130

polarity in, 140
self-healing in, 78
spiritual development in, 121
Tao in, 29
Taoist medicine, 224
Tao of Physics, The (Capra), 126
Tao Te Ching, 229
Teilhard de Chardin, Pierre, 217
Ten Commandments, 20, 160
Teresa, Mother, 128–30
Thich Nhat Hanh, 186–87, 217
Thich Quang Duc, 148
thoughts, 74, 184
three golden keys to spirituality, 4–6
three-hundred-and-sixty-degree
feedback process, 98
Tolle, Eckhart, 159–60
Tonglen ("giving and taking"),
197–98
transformational process, 122–23
transformation of negative energy,
197
tree of life, 74

U
unconditional positive regard,
173–74
UNESCO, 16
United Nations, 10, 16
Declaration of Human Rights,
19–20
universe, as forgiving, 201
unknowing
God and, 27–29
in psychotherapy, 188

Index

religions and, 146
   yielding to, 27, 115–16
unworthiness, 45–46, 201
Upanishads, 216, 229

V

values
   accusation of lacking, 17–18
   clarification and reiteration of,
      161–65
   green, 22
   holistic, 20–21
   in new spirituality, 17–18, 24,
      159–62
   personal statement of, 19
   religions and, 160–61
   shared, 18–21
Varieties of Religious Experience,
   The (James), 46
vibration
   affecting world, 183–84
   in organizations, 189
   of our presence, 181
   as service, 182–85
Vipassana, 109
visualization, 58–59, 70
vitality, 84
Vivekananda, 16
voices, hearing, 133–34

W

Walsch, Neale Donald, 64

watching. *See also* observation
   as core skill, 56, 72–75
   kindness to self and, 6–8, 72–75,
      103–4, 201
   in meditaton practice, 109
Web of Life (Capra), 30
well-being, 64
Wholeness and the Implicate Order
   (Bohm), (30)
Willoughby, Brian L. B., 1
Wilson, Edmund, 62
"witness consciousness," 89
wonder
   of child, 207
   in spiritual connection, 3, 5–6,
      27, 49, 62, 80, 181–82
World Parliament of Religions, 16,
   229
worthiness, 46

Y

yielding
   as core skill, 56, 76–78
   in Eucharist, 59
   in self-reflection, 104
yin and yang, 140, 142–44
yoga, 182, 184

Z

Zen, 109
Zukav, Gary, 126

Quest Books

217.
202.96.

encourages open-minded inquiry into
world religions, philosophy, science, and the arts
in order to understand the wisdom of the ages,
respect the unity of all life, and help people explore
individual spiritual self-transformation.

Its publications are generously supported by
The Kern Foundation,
a trust committed to Theosophical education.

Quest Books is the imprint of
the Theosophical Publishing House,
a division of the Theosophical Society in America.
For information about programs, literature,
on-line study, membership benefits, and international centers,
see www.theosophical.org
or call 800-669-1571 or (outside the U.S.) 630-668-1571.

Related Quest Titles

Beyond Religion, by David N. Elkins

Breathe into Being, by Dennis Lewis

The Brightened Mind, by Ajahn Sumano Bhikkhu

Feng Shui for the Body, by Daniel Santos

Growing into God, by John Mabry

The Meditative Path, by John Cianciosi

ProcessMind, by Arnold Mindell

To order books or a complete Quest catalog,
call 800-669-9425 or (outside the U.S.) 630-665-0130.

128 on
136